THE
collaborative
SALE

THE
collaborative
SALE

Solution Selling
in a Buyer-Driven World

KEITH M. EADES
TIMOTHY T. SULLIVAN

WILEY

For general information about our other products and services, please contact our Customer
Care Department within the United States at (800) 762-2974, outside the United States at
(317) 572-3993 or fax (317) 572-4002.

Wiley publishes in a variety of print and electronic formats and by print-on-demand.
Some material included with standard print versions of this book may not be included in
e-books or in print-on-demand. If this book refers to media such as a CD or DVD that is
not included in the version you purchased, you may download this material at
http://booksupport.wiley.com. For more information about Wiley products, visit
www.wiley.com.

ISBN 978-1-118-87242-0 (cloth); ISBN 978-1-118-87235-2 (ebk);
ISBN 978-1-118-87237-6 (ebk)

Printed in the United States of America

10 9 8 7 6 5 4 3 2 1

Dedicated to sales and marketing professionals, who commit themselves to improve their performance and contribute to their customers' success.
To our Sales Performance International family, who commit themselves every day to helping improve our clients' business results.
To our families, friends, and mentors who support, encourage, and allow us to travel the world in pursuit of our dreams.
To teachers globally that help educate, train, mentor, and coach us. It is through their love for leaning and giving to others that we achieve.
To the men and women in the armed services around the world, who put themselves in harm's way to protect our freedoms.

CONTENTS

FOREWORD

Buyer behavior has evolved and will continue to evolve through time. The more information buyers have access to, the less dependent they are on traditional sources of information—salespeople. Thanks to the Internet and the wealth of information it provides, buyers are more informed and more comfortable evaluating options on their own. As a result, buyers are more knowledgeable and more empowered than ever before.

Anything or anyone that does not add value to their buying process is eliminated, including high-pressure or situationally unknowledgeable salespeople. Buyers are never again going to relinquish power, or control of their buying process, to aggressive sellers who do not have their best interest at heart.

Further, we live in a world of uncertainty, with more unpredictability than ever before. Global economic uncertainties and the recent global recessions have made individual buyers as well as the companies they represent realize, perhaps once and for all, that they must see results and maximize their return on investment in every purchase. This means buyers are more cautious than ever and they are acutely aware of the risks of making bad decisions. In order to spread the risk, they involve many more people and often form buying committees in their rigorous evaluations. If today's buyers aren't convinced about the results and the value of a purchase, they simply choose to do nothing at all.

Due to these trends, sales professionals must adapt. The good news is that I see a great transformation taking place globally with sales professionals as they work to adapt to the new buyers. In fact, my firm, ES Research Group, which analyzes trends in selling practices and conducts independent evaluations of sales training companies, is seeing sellers achieve great results when they adapt to the new buying trends.

To succeed today, sellers need to be worthy collaborators with these knowledgeable buyers. No longer can sellers drive and control the sale; buyers are too empowered and savvy. Sellers must align with where the buyers are in their buying process and collaborate with them in an open and transparent manner. The sellers who do this are winning business and they are transforming selling forever. I truly believe this, and our research backs this up.

We surveyed 239 buy-side and 352 sell-side negotiators at the end of 2012, and asked them identical questions about the buying-selling process. When our researchers asked how respondents expect the environment to change in the near future, a strong majority of both said that they believe that buyers and sellers must and will become more collaborative over the next three years.

Our firm has been tracking and reporting on Sales Performance International (SPI) for seven years, and we have always rated it among the leading firms in the sales training and sales performance industry. Keith Eades and Tim Sullivan are two of SPI's thought leaders, and they share a passion for raising the quality of the sales profession. SPI has been best known for its methodology, Solution Selling®, which has been adopted by more than a million people all over the world. In many respects, that methodology has always been about effective collaboration with buyers. Keith and Tim have taken a close look at the recent changes in buyer behavior, evaluated the tenets of Solution Selling, and developed a modern view of what effective sellers need to do to succeed in today's world. The result is this book, *The Collaborative Sale*.

The Collaborative Sale introduces three new sales personae (Micro-Marketer, Visualizer, and Value Driver) that enable sellers to be more effective with today's savvy and informed buyers. The foundational competency behind the three new personae is called situational fluency. This competency allows sellers to engage buyers in multiple ways—through conversations on social media outlets like LinkedIn, Facebook, or Twitter or in direct conversations with buyers when trying to create, enhance, or reengineer their visions.

To sell with the transparency *The Collaborative Sale* proposes may be challenging for some sellers and their organizations. I feel strongly that today's buyers are demanding transparency and are demanding that sellers add value to their buying process from the moment they are engaged.

The Collaborative Age of Selling is now upon us. *The Collaborative Sale* will help you make the transition.

Dave Stein
Founder and CEO
ES Research Group, Inc.

PREFACE

Published in November 2003, *The New Solution Selling* quickly became required reading for many sales, sales management, and marketing professionals around the world. With over 300,000 copies sold, the book became a best seller and one of the most popular business books on the topic of sales and marketing. It still sells well today, more than 10 years after its debut.

However, propelled by the Internet and innovations in collaborative technologies, buyer behavior has changed significantly—some may even say radically—since 2003. In addition, the Millennial generation has arrived on the scene, bringing significant change to buying patterns as well. These changes in buyer behavior affect how we must market and sell in profound and highly disruptive ways. The reason for writing *The Collaborative Sale* is to address many of these significant changes in buyer behavior.

While writing this book about sales collaboration, I am also finalizing the architectural plans for my company's new international headquarters. What I've learned about the importance of sales collaboration throughout my career prompted me to ask our architect to design every aspect of our new space to foster collaboration among our associates and with our clients. Our open work spaces, impromptu meeting areas, innovation rooms, and even the height of the office walls are all designed to help people get more done through collaboration, and to enjoy themselves more while doing so.

I can't overemphasize the need for effective collaboration in this modern age. Effective selling is now a collaborative effort between equals—buyers and sellers—focused on an optimum result. Unfortunately, selling is viewed too often as an us-versus-them endeavor. But it doesn't need to be that way. This book, by my colleague Tim Sullivan and me, is our contribution to stemming the tides of disunity and mistrust.

The word *collaborate* is based on the Latin word *collaborare*, which means "to labor together." Each year, Sales Performance International works with more than 200 corporate clients to assess, train, and enable more than 25,000 sales and marketing professionals to "labor together" with buyers to solve their business problems. We have captured in this book much of what we've learned from our clients about sales collaboration.

Social scientists have demonstrated that even though insight feels like a solitary exercise, it is actually rooted in collaboration. We discovered a recent academic study that shows that a group of average people who collaborate effectively can solve problems more quickly than an expert acting alone.

Time after time, we've seen that sellers who successfully align their products, services, and capabilities with buyers' problems, critical business issues, and opportunities will elevate their status in the eyes of their customers. They will rise from "vendor" to "trusted partner," enabling higher levels of trust and collaboration. As a matter of fact, buyers often ask their trusted partners to collaborate on new ideas and will regularly write specifications and even requests for proposals (RFPs) and tenders around their capabilities.

And yes, sellers can achieve highly trusted status no matter what they sell. Some of our clients work in highly regulated monopolies, while others sell commodities like fuel, rocks, and financial investments; most fall somewhere in between, selling differentiated products or solutions in a competitive marketplace. But they all attain high levels of trust and credibility with customers by collaborating effectively and adding value in every interaction.

The Collaborative Sale removes barriers to collaboration by providing sellers with the processes, methods, tools, and skills they need, as well as the specific sales personae that they should play, when working with the new buyers.

I hope that you will not only enjoy our book, but will also let us know how you have put it to use to collaborate with your customers. Please drop us a note at www.thecollaborativesale.com or www.spisales.com with your story.

And if you will come visit us in our new headquarters, I'll treat you to a cup of coffee and take you for a tour. I hope you'll take me up on my offer.

Keith Eades
CEO and Founder
Sales Performance International, LLC

ACKNOWLEDGMENTS

T*he Collaborative Sale* is the result of our research and our work with our global clients, who are always challenging us to discover better ways to equip their sales teams to achieve maximum performance. To all of our clients, we thank you for the opportunity to make a difference in your businesses.

We also thank our colleagues at Sales Performance International (SPI), especially Robert Kear, Jimmy Touchstone, Brandon Uttley, Steve Smith, Jon Roy, Mike Racel, Dave Christofaro, Ken Cross, Grant Cox, Andy Smith, Mac McLaughlin, Phil McCrory, Jurgen Heyman, Steven Vantongelen, Sean DesNoyer, and Doug Handy. Their insights and contributions to this book have been enormous. Our thanks go also to Andrea Cinq-Mars and Leigh Anne Zeitouni for their help with graphics and aesthetic advice. And thanks also to the world's greatest assistant, Sandra Albertson.

We interviewed many clients and industry experts to identify and validate current trends and best practices in selling, which have been included in this book's contents. We would especially like to thank Alan Cline, Rob Ritchie, Bill Williams, David Ivester, David Quebbemann, Perry Santia, Bruce Balthaser, Harry Kelly, Alex Boss, Stefaan van Hooydonk, Robert Chesney, Dave Stein, Peter Ostrow, Jim Ninivaggi, and Jim Dickie for their time and willingness to share their experiences and observations.

We give special thanks and recognition to Tamela Rich, a talented writer, for her contributions to this book. Tamela has a special gift of getting the most out of other writers. And thanks to Judy Anderson, a talented teacher, for her edits and for introducing us to *The Spyglass*.

Our gratitude goes to Matthew Holt and Shannon Vargo at John Wiley & Sons, who enthusiastically supported this project and were instrumental in the book's publication.

Finally, we thank our families, especially our wives, Margie Eades and Jane Sullivan, for their enduring support and inspiration.

DEFINITIONS

Throughout this book, we use the following words to express certain general concepts. These words could have different nuances of meaning depending on the industry and specific application in which they might be used. For the purposes of this book, we have tried to maintain consistency in the use of these terms. To avoid confusion, we define them here for the reader.

- **Buyer**—A person who is involved in the evaluation or decision to purchase a product, service, or solution. This could be someone acting as an individual or as part of a group. The buyer could be of any title, function, or rank—this role is not limited to a dedicated purchasing or procurement professional.

- **Buyer 2.0**—Modern buying behaviors characterized by an abundance of research and information gathering, engaging sellers much later in their buying process and having a high aversion to risk.

- **Customer/client**—A buyer with whom a seller has a prior business relationship, either individually or with that buyer's organization.

- **Persona**—A character role that a seller needs to assume and/or play, in order to align with Buyer 2.0 processes and concerns.

- **Prospect**—A buyer with whom a seller does not have a prior business relationship, either individually or with that buyer's organization.

- **Sales collaboration**—Buyers and sellers bringing their ideas and perspectives together using a transparent and commonly understood structure, in shared physical or virtual space, to solve mutually recognized problems or to benefit from identified opportunities, and to create measurable value.

- **Seller**—A person who interacts with a buyer to help the buyer make an informed purchase decision. This could be an individual acting alone or as part of a selling team. This person could be selling primarily over the telephone, in face-to-face interactions, through web collaboration, or in some combination of inter-personal interaction modalities. A seller could be an employee representative, an independent agent, or a business partner. In this book, we use the term *seller* universally for consistency. This term is interchangeable with salesperson, sales professional, salesman, saleswoman, and so on.

Part I
Foundations of the Collaborative Sale

1 "The Story" and What's behind *The Collaborative Sale*

Jon was a sales superstar, and the rapidly growing company we'll call "ExyRisk" couldn't wait to get him on board as a rainmaker. Jon's success in selling technology solutions into the financial services industry, coupled with his Wharton MBA, made him a coveted midcareer hire for ExyRisk, a developer of financial risk modeling software based in the San Francisco area. Recently purchased by a private equity firm, the four-year-old company was under intense pressure to perform, and it needed top sales talent.

But within six months of being hired, no one was more surprised than Jon when he realized he couldn't close sales in his new job.

After he joined ExyRisk, Jon did what he had always done—he reached out to his network to arrange introductions to senior-level prospects. When he met with them, potential buyers were intrigued by ExyRisk's capabilities, but he couldn't get more than a couple of his prospects to agree to a demo. Their reasons varied but were based on one of two themes. The first was: "We've got a project on the horizon that this might be a good fit for, but right now we have to execute what's on our plate." The other was: "Our budgets are on lockdown, so there's no need to waste your time giving us a demo on something we can't buy."

His best lead was an insurance brokerage that specialized in severe weather modeling to set risk pools. Jon saw an opportunity to partner with the broker who would resell ExyRisk's software with various applications that the broker offered. He flew to New York for the annual Risk Management Conference where the broker was facilitating a panel discussion, and the two Wharton grads had breakfast the next morning.

After the conference meeting, ExyRisk's CEO reached Jon on his phone as he was boarding his return flight. "He just doesn't get it," Jon said of the broker. "He's telling me they've got to focus on their core offerings before they start working with partners."

The CEO had been hearing a lot of this sort of thing from Jon. It seemed like the world according to Jon was filled with nearsighted and self-absorbed prospects who didn't know a good thing when they saw it.

As the CEO spoke with Jon, a private equity partner and board member was in the office listening in. Leaning into the speakerphone, she said, "Jon, this is Nancy. Can you tell me a little bit about the broker's business problems?"

Jon shot back, "I'm offering him something that will increase revenue from his firm's current customer base. Who doesn't want that?"

Nancy bristled. "Okay, then, what do you know about his revenue problems?"

Jon replied, "He needs a helluva lot more. Who doesn't? Listen, they're making the announcement to turn off our cell phones. I've got to go."

Nancy said, "Jon, I'm going to meet you at the airport this afternoon, and we're going to come up with a new sales approach."

Jon got a text from Nancy telling him to meet him at the Delta Sky Club. Walking through the airport, he called his wife to update her on his revised schedule, and swiftly changed the subject when she asked him if something was wrong.

The Sky Club attendant pointed to the room that Nancy had reserved and Jon drew a deep breath. Into the lion's den, he thought as he opened the door.

Nancy was on ExyRisk's board because she, like Jon, had a background in finance and technology. Unlike Jon, she came up through the ranks as an analyst, so he wasn't sure what expertise she had to offer when it came to making sales.

Nancy looked up from her laptop, stood to shake Jon's hand, and said, "I'm glad your plane was on time. Mine leaves in about three hours." Closing the lid on her laptop and turning her phone to vibrate, she said, "Let's get down to business, shall we?" and sat down.

"Sure thing," he said in a neutral tone, tossing his backpack into the blue club chair by the window and taking his seat at the faux granite table across from Nancy. It was his first meeting with her, although he had been introduced to her the last time she was in town for a board meeting.

"Jon, I reviewed your resume as I was waiting for your plane. You've had a good run working with a series of high-tech companies. Not to sound like I'm interviewing you for the job all over again, but tell me why you've changed jobs every two or three years."

"Wow, Nancy, that's quite an opening volley," he quipped. Smoothing the creases in his khakis, he continued, "I'm not a job-hopper, just a guy who knows how to manage his career and work his way up. I was always recruited away. I'm good at what I do. I'm just not sure what's wrong with ExyRisk."

Nancy smiled out of the left corner of her mouth. "I expected you to say something like that. And I believe that you believe that story."

She leaned back in her chair and said, "I've had this conversation with half a dozen other business development people over the past year. Here's how it goes every time. Looking at the companies you represented and when you were with each one, I know that you've succeeded with strong winds at your back."

Jon opened his mouth, but Nancy raised a finger to stop him from saying something they might both regret.

"You joined the companies when they had innovative products and little competition, which meant you were able to focus on their unique differentiators. Your numbers were strong, and the next company recruited you away. Nothing to be ashamed of in your track record."

Jon closed his mouth as she continued.

"I'm pointing out that ExyRisk doesn't have the same kind of product differentiation that you've always sold. To be able to sell ExyRisk, you're going to have to be savvier about who you're selling to and why they're buying."

"Who I'm selling to? I'm selling software to financial services companies."

"I see," she said, resting her arms on the table and clasping her hands. "Let's talk about this insurance broker. What have you done to quantify in hard dollars the value the broker could realize with ExyRisk? Could you cite other customers like this broker and what they've achieved?"

"No, because this is the first insurance broker I've met with," he said. "I've always been successful in showing clients what the product does and then brainstorming how they could use it. It's been a collaborative thing once I get the demo. But this is the first product I haven't been able to demo."

"Oh, Jon, I like where you're going with the collaboration theme, but you're just left of center. When you tell a prospect 'let's brainstorm,' you're saying that you aren't sure how you can help them.

Buyers are protective of their time, which is money. Remember," she said, lowering her voice, "you're not selling them something they've never *ever* seen before."

Jon thought for a few moments. "So, what should I do?" he asked.

The Collaborative Sale

Like Jon, many sales professionals are struggling today, finding opportunities harder to win, buyers more reluctant to engage, and consistent results more difficult to produce. Many sellers perceive that buyers have changed in some fundamental ways, and traditional ways of selling don't succeed like they once did.

Buyers have indeed changed, in some dramatic ways. They are now much more informed than ever before. Their reliance on sellers for information has declined greatly. At the same time, buyers are more cautious and risk averse. This makes them harder for sellers to access, and more difficult to persuade to buy.

Buyers' expectations of sellers have also changed. They demand that sellers bring valuable expertise and a higher level of work commitment and professionalism than ever before.

Many sellers will falter in this more challenging environment. But many can still succeed if they can align with buyers' higher expectations. Those who recognize that selling is now a collaborative effort between equals—buyers and sellers, working together toward an optimum result—will be the successful sales professionals, both today and through the next decade.

This book, *The Collaborative Sale*, represents our latest findings about effective sales practices collected from our research and experience with hundreds of our clients. It builds upon the foundation of our well-known methodology, Solution Selling®, which we documented in our previous books, *The New Solution Selling* and *The Solution*

Selling Fieldbook. That methodology was built upon the foundational principle of a buyer-aligned sales process at its core. As a result, it has proven to be uniquely adaptable to changes in buyer behavior over the past decade, providing over one million sales professionals with an integrated system for achieving consistently improved sales results.

However, when we studied the latest trends in buyer behavior, which we document in the next chapter, we realized that the dynamic between buyers and sellers was changing in very profound ways. We discovered that the most important factor in successful selling has become the ability of sellers to collaborate with their buyers, at every stage of the buying process.

The good news was that Solution Selling always included effective collaboration principles and tools as an integral part of its design. However, we also discovered that some new methods to collaborate with buyers could be added, and others could be further improved.

For over a year, we experimented intensely with sales collaboration approaches, tools, techniques, and methods, working with various clients. The result is a newly modernized version of effective sales methodology, which we now call *The Collaborative Sale: Solution Selling in a Buyer-Driven World.* This approach has proven to be extraordinarily well-tuned to help sellers align with the demands of modern buyers, and to differentiate themselves—not just by what they sell but, more importantly, by *how* they sell to buyers.

The principles of *The Collaborative Sale* are based firmly in validated research and real-world application. For example, an independent 2013 study by the RAIN Group found that the two most important characteristics of high-performing sellers were the ability to provide buyers with new ideas and perspectives and the ability to collaborate with buyers.[1]

---

[1]Mike Schultz and John Doerr, "New Sales Research: What Sales Winners Do Differently," RAIN Group, April 2013.

Additional independent research by ES Research Group shows that a large majority of both buyers and sellers believe that sales negotiations are becoming more collaborative, and will continue to grow more collaborative over the next three years.[2] That same research shows that buyers and sellers agree strongly on what impacts their interactions positively, including:

- Buying and selling organizations working together to help shape solution requirements *before* they are finalized

- Quantifying measurable value to establish a baseline understanding for contract negotiations and purchase decisions

- Intentionally involving customer stakeholders, including users of the proposed products and/or services, to help educate the purchasing team on buying criteria, value points, and other factors.

What Is Sales Collaboration?

The dictionary defines collaboration simply as: "To work jointly with others or together, especially in an intellectual endeavor."[3] While this definition describes the action of collaborating, it does not really explain why people would do so. A more insightful definition can be found in Evan Rosen's book, *The Culture of Collaboration*: "Working together to create value while sharing virtual and physical space."[4] The intent of collaboration is to create new value for the participants that could not otherwise be realized by acting individually. Rosen also

---

[2]Dave Stein, "The State of Sales and Purchasing," ES Research Group, November 2012. Accessed December 1, 2013, at www.esresearch.com/e/home/document.php?dA=ESR_sales_purchasing. Also corroborated with a personal interview with Dave Stein, conducted October 1, 2013.

[3]"Collaborate," Merriam-Webster.com. Accessed November 13, 2013, at www.merriam-webster.com/dictionary/collaborate.

[4]Evan Rosen, *The Culture of Collaboration: Maximizing Time, Talent and Tools to Create Value in the Global Economy* (San Francisco: Red Ape Pub., 2009).

recognizes that collaboration can occur both in person and virtually. Technology enables people to connect and collaborate in a variety of ways that do not require physical proximity.

Many people take for granted that collaboration will produce better results than individuals acting alone. They assume that bringing together a group with different ideas and perspectives can help to foster more innovative ways of looking at a problem or potential opportunity, but this is not always what happens.

Research by Leigh Thompson, PhD, a professor at the Kellogg School of Management at Northwestern University and author of *Creative Conspiracy: The New Rules of Breakthrough Collaboration*,[5] found that individuals working independently on a problem before coming together as a team generated almost three times more ideas, and higher-quality ideas, than just a group brainstorming together. In addition, other research by psychologists shows that the most productive forms of collaboration are not free-form interactions, but those governed by well-defined structures and commonly understood processes.[6]

These research findings provide two important lessons for sellers:

1. To collaborate effectively with a buyer, sellers must first understand the buyer's issues and develop ideas and hypotheses on how best to address those issues.

2. Sellers who use a transparent and readily understood structure for collaborating with buyers produce better outcomes than those who engage reactively with no or poorly defined processes.

---

[5]Leigh L. Thompson, *Creative Conspiracy: The New Rules of Breakthrough Collaboration* (Boston: Harvard Business School Publishing, 2013).
[6]P. B. Paulus, T. Nakui, V. R. Brown, and V. L. Putman, "Effects of Task Instructions and Brief Breaks on Brainstorming," *Group Dynamics: Theory, Research and Practice* 10, no. 3 (2006): 206–219.

Sales collaboration is therefore more than simply working with buyers to fulfill common interests. It is buyers and sellers bringing their ideas and perspectives together using a transparent and commonly understood structure, in shared physical or virtual space, to solve mutually recognized problems or to benefit from identified opportunities, and to create measurable value.

Most sellers are unaware of how much they could collaborate with buyers, and as a result they miss opportunities to connect with new buyers to demonstrate their expertise, jointly develop visions of solutions, and provide exceptional value. By embracing a collaborative sales approach, sellers can:

- Improve the quantity and quality of sales pipelines by creating, finding, and developing more opportunities.

- Engage with prospective buyers earlier in their purchase evaluations.

- Differentiate themselves from alternative options by demonstrating thought leadership to buyers.

- Sell openly and transparently by sharing a collaborative approach and intent with buyers, and further differentiate from other sellers.

- Develop higher levels of credibility and trust with buyers by documenting and posting useful information on a dedicated collaborative portal—and also equipping buyers to support a recommended solution within their own organizations.

- Work more effectively with buying committees by enabling all of them to participate actively throughout the purchase process.

- Guide buyers to a decision by providing a useful approach for each buying group to apply, shared in secure online collaboration sites.

- Codevelop mutually agreed-upon estimates of value with buyers, providing compelling reasons for buyers to act.

- Decide when to stop or qualify out of an opportunity in the best mutual interests of both the seller and the buyer.

Sellers who work with buyers using a collaborative sales approach produce improved results, for both themselves and their customers. This collaborative approach requires new skills and competencies, but it can be learned and mastered by most sales professionals. They only need to know the way. *The Collaborative Sale* shows how.

2 Solution Selling Meets the New Buyer

More than one million sales, sales management, and marketing professionals around the world count on and use our branded sales methodology known as Solution Selling®.[1] It enables sellers to sell more, helps marketing to create awareness and generate more leads, and provides management with visibility and predictability—all while better managing buyers' expectations and creating higher levels of customer satisfaction. In simple terms, Solution Selling works by delivering consistent business results for sellers and their buyers.

As owners of the methodology, Sales Performance International (SPI) works diligently to enhance and maintain Solution Selling's

---

[1] Solution Selling® is a registered trademark of Sales Performance International, LLC (SPI), and pertains to the exclusive methodology and related tool set for engaging with buyers and effective sales execution. For more information about Solution Selling, see our published works: Keith M. Eades, *The New Solution Selling: The Revolutionary Sales Process That Is Changing the Way People Sell* (New York: McGraw-Hill, 2003), and Keith M. Eades, James N. Touchstone, and Timothy T. Sullivan, *The Solution Selling Fieldbook* (New York: McGraw-Hill, 2005). SPI reserves all rights to the proper use of the Solution Selling trademark, worldwide.

relevancy in the marketplace. Our work with clients, our research, and the knowledge we gain from industry analysts enable us to keep the methodology current with buying and selling trends. In spite of this, some pundits have written that "Solution Selling is dead." This couldn't be further from the truth. Regardless of whether the pundits' statements are made out of ignorance, jealousy, or incorrect assumptions of what is contained in Solution Selling, they are simply wrong.

From its inception, Solution Selling has always been based on the philosophy that a *solution* is an answer to a business problem or opportunity. And if sellers are in the solutions business, they must help buyers discover problems or opportunities, consultatively diagnose the issues, and then create or reengineer visions of solutions, determine the value of the proposed ideas, reach mutual agreement, and track business results. This philosophy, and the approach based on it, is as relevant today as the day it was first introduced. Solution Selling changed the dynamic between buyers and sellers by requiring sellers to engage consultatively with buyers about their problems and opportunities, rather than about the products or services the sellers represent.

The genesis of Solution Selling started in technology-related industries. The tech boom in the 1980s and 1990s created an array of new, complex business products that made fresh demands on sellers, requiring new knowledge and skills beyond a basic understanding of product offerings. To sell these new capabilities successfully, sellers had to become adept at diagnosing buyers' business problems and helping to shape visions of applicable solutions. Solution Selling provides the skills, process, methods, and supporting sales and marketing tools to do this consistently.

Since the initial introduction of Solution Selling, markets have become increasingly global and competitive. Both the desire and the necessity to preserve margins by selling higher-value solutions have permeated virtually all industries. As a result, we have seen demand for Solution Selling expand dramatically into a broad array of industries, including advanced manufacturing, construction materials, health care, medical devices, logistics, business services, telecommunications, financial services, office products, and even some levels of retail. Our clients all tell us that it is increasingly difficult to maintain product or service superiority over competitors, and therefore they must differentiate in how they engage with buyers. Solution Selling enabled them to do so—and continues to enable them to do so today.

AberdeenGroup conducted two independent surveys in 2011 and 2012 of organizations that implemented sales training projects. In both years, users of SPI's Solution Selling methodology reported higher levels of quota attainment, more repeat business from customers, faster time to productivity for new hires, and larger average sales size, relative to all other alternative training programs.[2] The data shows that Solution Selling enables sellers to achieve best-in-class performance levels faster and more consistently.

Based on the continued success of our clients, and on the persistently increasing adoption and use of Solution Selling as a differentiating factor, the issue is not whether the methodology is still relevant; rather, it is why it continues to be so. The reason is found at its very core: Solution Selling is designed to help sellers understand and align with how buyers buy.

However, we cannot deny that buyer behavior has changed in substantial ways as a result of the Internet, new buyer demographics, increased globalization of markets, and international economic trends. It is fortuitous that Solution Selling's essential design has enabled it to reflect these behavior changes very well, but it would be folly to

---

[2]Peter Ostrow, "Sales Performance Optimization 2013: Aligning the Right People, Processes, and Tools," *Research Brief*, AberdeenGroup, February 2, 2013. Accessed December 1, 2013, at www.aberdeen.com/Aberdeen-Library/8347/RB-sales-performance-optimization.aspx.

proclaim that the methodology cannot be further improved to accommodate and align with today's buyers. That is the central purpose of this book: to show how Solution Selling meets and aligns with the new buyer, and how it enables sellers to be more productive and successful.

The Emergence of the New Buyer—Buyer 2.0

Based on both independent research and our experience with clients, we have observed four fundamental changes in buyer behavior that have accelerated greatly since 2011:

1. Buyers are delaying the involvement of sellers in their buying process.
2. More people are involved in purchase decisions; buying by committee is more common than ever before.
3. Buyers have developed a higher aversion to risk, resulting in more decisions to do nothing or to simply maintain the status quo.
4. Buyers are asserting more formalized control over their purchasing processes and are demanding greater seller transparency.

These changes in behavior have become increasingly pervasive, and are rapidly becoming the norm. We call the buyers who exhibit these behaviors "Buyer 2.0." This new standard of buyer behavior is a result of three principal factors: increased information access, the rise of the Millennial generation, and the persistent unpredictability of global economic trends.

The Effect of Information Access on Buyer 2.0 Behavior

Buyers now wait longer than they used to before talking to sellers directly. A 2010 DemandGen Report study on buyer behavior found that 79 percent of business-to-business buyers do not talk to sellers until they have performed their own independent research—and more than half (51 percent) engage with sellers only after establishing a preferred short list of vendors.[3]

Forrester Research states, "Although it varies greatly with product complexity and market maturity, today's buyers might be anywhere from *two-thirds to 90 percent* of the way through their journey before they reach out to [a] vendor."[4]

Increased information access is the driver of this fundamental change in buyer behavior. Before the Internet became widely available, sellers controlled most of the flow of information to buyers. If an organization needed a product or service, they contacted several potential vendors, met with sellers, and made their decisions on the information they received from each potential supplier. Sellers provided almost all of the messages and information that purchasers used to make their buying decisions.

Today, however, buyers have easy access to information about potential solutions for their problems. They can simply log on to the Internet and conduct a keyword search. With a little more effort, buyers can learn all about potential suppliers from many sources, including industry analysts, consultants, web bloggers, and customers of those suppliers and their direct competitors. They can find online forums where these groups congregate, and can open dialogues with them.

Buyers are no longer dependent on sellers to provide them with information. In fact, they can find more useful sources of information to form opinions and start an evaluation for potential purchases without any help from a seller's organization.

---

[3] *Breaking Out of the Funnel: A Look Inside the Mind of the New Generation of BtoB Buyer.* DemandGen Report, sponsored by Genius.com, March 24, 2010. Accessed December 1, 2013, at www.demandgenreport.com/industry-resources/research/430-breaking-out-of-the-funnel-a-look-inside-the-mind-of-the-new-generation-of-btob-buyer.html.
[4] Lori Wizdo, "Buyer Behavior Helps B2B Marketers Guide the Buyer's Journey," *Forrester Blogs*, Forrester Research, October 4, 2012. Accessed December 1, 2013.

This behavior shift should not surprise anyone. In fact, it was predicted in 1999, when Rick Levine, Chris Locke, Doc Searls, and David Weinberger published their *Cluetrain Manifesto*.[5] These futurists and industry observers correctly suggested that the Internet would change buyer behavior in fundamental ways.

"Markets are conversations," they said. "A powerful global conversation has begun. Through the Internet, people are discovering and inventing new ways to share relevant knowledge with blinding speed. As a direct result, markets are getting smarter—and getting smarter faster than most companies."

This fundamental shift in buyer behavior has been further confirmed by a growing number of supporting industry research findings:

- The industry analyst firm SiriusDecisions conducted research in 2013 and found that online searches are executives' first course of action when researching a potential purchase. They also discovered that, for most business-to-business purchases, buyers do not rely on suppliers' salespeople to provide them with educational information.[6]

- A previous research study by Forbes Insights and Google also showed that executives prefer to conduct their own research on possible purchase alternatives, using mostly online resources to do so.[7]

---

[5]Rick Levine, Christopher Locke, Doc Searls, and David Weinberger, *The Cluetrain Manifesto: The End of Business as Usual* (New York: Perseus, 2011). Also: "People of Earth . . . ," *The Cluetrain Manifesto*, 2013, www.cluetrain.com.
[6]Megan Heuer, "Where Sales and Marketing Meet," *SiriusDecisions Blog*, SiriusDecisions, July 3, 2013. Accessed December 1, 2013, at www.siriusdecisions.com/blog/three-myths-of-the-67-percent-statistic/.
[7]"The Rise of the Digital C-Suite: How Executives Locate and Filter Business Information," *Forbes*, June 2009. Accessed December 1, 2013, at www.forbes.com/forbesinsights/digital_csuite/index.html. Based on an exclusive survey of 354 top executives at large U.S. companies with annual sales greater than $1 billion, conducted in association with Google.

- AberdeenGroup, another analyst firm that conducts research on business best practices, confirmed in a 2011 survey that "by the time a potential buyer is identified, qualified and engaged, the prospect may already be well into their research and decision-making process" because buyers conduct their own online research in advance of contacting any sellers.[8]

- In a Buyersphere 2013 study of business-to-business purchasing trends, the first choice of executive buyers for information on potential suppliers is browsing their websites.[9]

- A 2013 Zogby Analytics study of over 1,000 buyers discovered that "Today's buyers are increasingly using the Internet to research, inquire about and purchase a variety of high-value products and services for both business and personal use. Most buyers are well-informed prior to engaging with vendors due to the amount of research they perform prior to contact."[10]

In 2011, we had the opportunity to observe a seller in action as he dealt with an active evaluation-stage buyer. He was presenting to a financial services firm that was interested in his company's customer relationship management (CRM) software application. We were

---

[8]Trip Kucera and Peter Ostrow, "The Marketing Executive's Agenda for 2012: Uncovering the Hidden Sales Cycle," AberdeenGroup, October 4, 2011. Accessed December 1, 2013, at www.aberdeen.com/Aberdeen-Library/7364/AI-marketing-agenda-technology.aspx.

[9]John Bottom, *The 2013 Buyersphere Report: The Industry's Favourite Expose of B2B Buyer Behaviour*, Base One, September 5, 2013. Accessed December 1, 2013, at www.baseone.co.uk/beyond/2013/09/the-2013-buyersphere-report-the-industrys-favourite-expose-of-b2b-buyer-beh.

[10]*Online Buyer Expectations*, Velocify, Autumn 2013. Accessed December 1, 2013, at http://pages.velocify.com/OnlineBuyerExpectations2.html?wp=109. An online survey of more than 1,000 adults in the United States who had submitted an online form requesting information or expressing interest in a product or service with a value of $1,000 or more. Commissioned by Velocify and PossibleNOW and conducted by Zogby Analytics.

looking forward to the meeting, as the salesperson was one of the top producers in the company and had a reputation as a polished speaker.

The meeting was attended by many of the company's executives, including the chief financial officer (CFO), who welcomed everyone and started the meeting by saying, "We've done a lot of research on your organization. We've reviewed your website, talked with several consultants, reviewed some reports by industry analysts—we've even chatted with a few of your customers. We're impressed and eager to make a decision, but we need to know if your application can do one important thing for our business."

The CFO briefly described the key capability that they wanted the application to perform. "If you can show us how you can address that issue, we can start working on a contract."

We were smiling, as we knew that the software could do exactly what the CFO asked. This was going to be easy for the salesperson—a slam dunk, as they say in basketball.

But that's when it all went wrong.

"Thank you," the seller replied. "I'd like to begin by telling you a little about our company." The seller then started his PowerPoint presentation, and proceeded to speak eloquently about his firm, the standards they complied with, their growth rate, their office locations, and their complete set of offerings and services.

After 30 minutes, it was clear that the customer team was getting annoyed. The CFO interrupted the seller in midsentence. "Look," he said, "we already know all about your company. We just need to answer this one question. Can we dispense with all of this background, and get to that?"

"I understand," the seller replied calmly. "I just have a few more slides first, and then we'll get to your issue."

The seller plowed ahead with his presentation, concluding, "And we'd very much want your business." But he never really addressed the

CFO's question. When asked again if he could speak to that issue, the salesperson simply said, "No, but I'm sure I can bring in a subject matter expert who can."

The meeting ended abruptly at that point. The seller didn't get the order.

Though that seller failed in many ways, he was simply following what he had been taught to do—lead with the company's strengths, explain the features and advantages in language the customer will understand, and ask for the order. And because he worked for a well-known, market-leading supplier, that approach was usually effective.

But in this case, the CFO and his team were already very well educated. They were insulted when the information that they already knew was forced upon them again.

The seller had made several bad assumptions, including acting as if the buyer was early in the purchasing process. The buyer was actually much further along, so the seller and buyer were completely out of alignment. As a result, he lost the opportunity to make the sale.

The Millennials Are Coming

The term *Millennial* is associated with people born between 1980 and the early 2000s. And to say they are different from baby boomers is an understatement. More than 10,000 baby boomers reach the retirement age of 65 each day in the United States alone. Millennials already make up 36 percent of the U.S. workforce; by 2020 they will be almost half of the workforce. (See Figure 2.1.)

Millennials behave differently than prior generations of workers:

- Sixty-four percent ask about social media policies during job interviews.

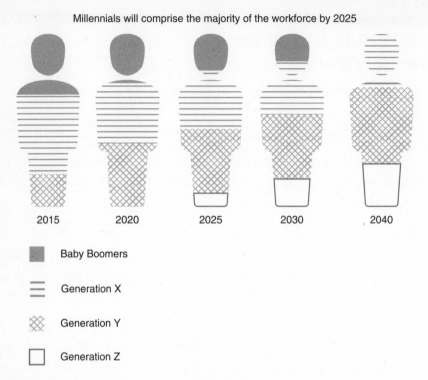

Figure 2.1   The Rise of the Millennials

- Sixty-five percent say that personal development was the most influential factor in choosing their job.

- Twenty-two percent say that training and development were the most valuable benefits of an employer.

- Millennials switch attention between media platforms an average of 27 times per hour.

- Forty-three percent have "liked" more than 20 brands on Facebook.

- One in three say they value "social media freedom" and "work mobility" over salary.

- Thirty percent started a business in college.

- Forty-three percent feel confident they could find another job if they lost or left their current one.

- Seventy percent of them plan to change jobs when the economy improves.

Millennial demographics are shaping buyer and seller behavior. Sales organizations will be forced to adapt and leverage new talents and perspectives. Collaboration skills will be essential when engaging with Millennial buyers. Seller transparency will be considered "table stakes" when dealing with Millennial buyers; they expect to be treated as equals throughout their buying process.

Because they are so technically savvy, Millennial buyers will set new standards for doing their own research. Not only do they engage sellers much later in the buying process, but they may not engage sellers at all. Sellers will need to interact with Millennial buyers through social media, in order to improve the chances of shaping their initial buying visions.

The Effect of Economic Uncertainty on Buyer 2.0 Behavior

No matter what buyers are thinking about purchasing, they invariably go through multiple buying phases during their buying process, and their concerns vary in importance in each phase and over time, as illustrated in Figure 2.2.

Most buying processes begin after some form of planning takes place, when buyers become aware of problems or potential opportunities that need to be addressed. After recognizing a business issue, buyers enter into the *determine needs* phase, where they are most concerned with identifying what is needed to address the issue and the potential cost or investment required to acquire what is needed. Once their needs are defined and initial budgets are determined (at least informally), their foremost concern shifts to the *evaluate alternatives*

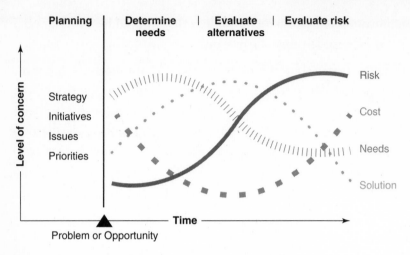

Figure 2.2   Buying Phases: Shifting Buyer Concerns

phase of their buying process, where they examine and compare different alternatives that could meet their requirements and budget expectations. Near the end of their buying process, after they have evaluated alternatives, buyers' concerns shift to the *evaluate risk* phase of their buying process, where they try to understand the level of risk in making a purchase decision. In this last phase, the cost or price of making a commitment once again becomes important in the minds of buyers.

These psychological buying phases—determining needs, evaluating alternatives, and evaluating risk—may happen very quickly for low-risk transactional purchases or take much longer for higher-risk, larger, or more important purchase decisions.

For example, something as trivial as buying a box of mints in the supermarket may simply be a question of deciding what type of mint might be most desired, looking at the different alternatives on the shelf for the closest fit, and then deciding if you have enough cash to make the purchase. This process may take only a few seconds to complete.

For larger or more important purchases, this process will take much longer. For example, a young couple may decide they'd rather build equity in a house than pay rent. Their initial list of needs may include a number of ideal requirements: three bedrooms, safe neighborhood, less than a 40-minute commute to and from work, two-car garage, convenience to shopping, good schools, and so on. They establish a budget for the price of a house and a monthly mortgage payment they can afford. Once these criteria have been set, they can then compare and evaluate alternatives.

In the past, this meant contacting a real estate broker for help. Today, however, most home buyers begin their search on the Internet, and conduct their own initial research. They will probably not contact a broker until they have a clear idea of what kind of home they want, and where they'd like it to be.

Many home buyers look at houses that are outside of their original budget. This is normal behavior for people going through the evaluation of alternatives phase, as it costs little other than an investment in time to look at a variety of different options.

Once they have narrowed their choices down to a couple of ideal options, buyers start to become more concerned about the risks of their buying decision.

Our home buyers may ask: Is this the best price for this house? How secure are our jobs? Can we afford this house if something happens to either of us? Can we make the monthly mortgage payments for the next 30 years? Only when they have answers to their questions about risk will our buyers move forward with a purchase commitment. Evaluating risk causes people to slow down their decision-making process, and maybe not make a decision at all.

For decades, this model of the psychology of buyers has remained consistent, except for one important aspect—for Buyer 2.0, who is buying in a period of sustained economic unpredictability, the level of concern about risk has been elevated throughout the buying process. When people cannot reliably predict what direction the economy is likely to take, and how those trends may affect their business and their organization, they hold on to cash in order to remain flexible and adaptable to uncertain conditions.

We see this unprecedented level of buyer concern about risk manifesting in several ways:

- *More thorough buyer evaluations, with more people involved in the buying process.* CSO Insights found in a 2013 study that over three-quarters of all business-to-business purchases included at least three people in the buying process, and only 3 percent of purchase decisions were made by one person.[11] More people involved in purchases means sellers must communicate with more people than ever before. Their conversations need to communicate value in different ways to each person, and they must navigate successfully through the politics of the customers' buying decision process, which can be complex and difficult to discern.

- *More buyer decisions to remain with the status quo.* CSO Insights also found that of all the opportunities that sellers forecast to close, nearly one-quarter (24 percent) result in no decision by the customer.[12] When buyers perceive a high amount of risk or they don't have a compelling reason to act that is greater than their perception of the risk, they typically opt not to buy at all. We often refer to this as losing to "No Decision Inc."

- *More involvement by formal procurement departments.* According to a global 2011 study by KPMG of procurement best practices, almost 60 percent of all business purchases were managed by formalized procurement departments, and this level is expected

---

[11] Jim Dickie, "2013 Sales Performance Optimization," *Sales Performance Optimization Report*, CSO Insights, Summer 2013. Accessed December 1, 2013, at www.csoinsights.com/Publications/Shop/Sales-Performance-Optimization.
[12] Ibid.

to increase, especially in larger, more mature businesses.[13] The role of formal purchasing departments is expanding beyond their initial goal of expense control to also include improvement of cash flow, managing supplier relationships, and mitigating purchasing risk. Sellers should not ignore the increasingly important role that formal purchasing departments play in buying decisions.

Buyer 2.0 versus Buyer 1.0

As previously discussed, with unprecedented access to information Buyer 2.0 is not so reliant on sellers to lead the buyer through the early stages of the buying process. Prior generations of buyers, whom we refer to as Buyer 1.0, were much more dependent on the seller for information, especially in the early buying phases of the buying process. The new buyers (Buyer 2.0) identify their own business issues, conduct research, reach out to peers, participate in blogs and forums, and attempt to determine their own needs and formulate a list of evaluation criteria. In many cases, the seller either is completely locked out of early buying process phases or is contacted only informally to help validate initial findings. (See Figure 2.3.)

As a result, in the emerging world of Buyer 2.0 behavior, sellers find themselves generally reacting to preestablished visions of solutions created by buyers, instead of helping buyers to identify critical business issues and then shaping solution visions for them. Buyer 2.0 now forms a hypothesis of the capabilities needed to address business issues before ever engaging with sellers.

The abundance of information available to buyers can put even the best sales professionals on the defensive—in a position of simply reacting and competing on price. The ability to sell the value of

---

[13]Richard Nixon, "The Power of Procurement," KPMG, February 21, 2012. Accessed December 1, 2013, at www.kpmg.com/global/en/issuesandinsights/articlespublications/pages/management-consulting-benchmarking.aspx.

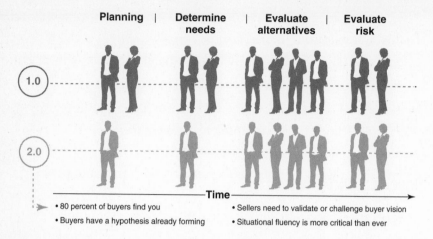

Figure 2.3   Buyer 1.0 versus Buyer 2.0 Engagement of Sellers

possible solutions is more critical now than ever. Sellers must be more agile to engage effectively with Buyer 2.0. Sellers who can adeptly capture and then enhance or reengineer a customer's vision of a solution now have a distinct edge. The new breed of informed buyers requires rethinking how sales process and sales methodologies are best structured and applied.

Adapting to the Buyer 2.0 Paradigm

For companies that strive to market and sell higher-value solutions, there are many potential ramifications of the Buyer 2.0 paradigm. Many organizations are reacting tactically to buyer behavior changes, using highly fragmented approaches without truly understanding what fundamental changes are happening and why they are occurring. This is akin to a doctor prescribing a remedy without first understanding the malady. In medicine, this is called malpractice; in sales, we call it recklessness. Here are a few examples:

- We've seen organizations invest heavily in product training, think-ing better understanding of their capabilities will enable sellers to have more meaningful conversations with buyers. Usually, this simply leads to more focus on product selling instead of understanding customer problems, and therefore to misalignment with Buyer 2.0.

- We've seen organizations attempt to address sales performance gaps by introducing new incentive compensation plans. But all too often the plans do not take the new normal of Buyer 2.0 behavior into account, leading to misalignment with buyers and poor results.

- We've seen organizations invest more heavily in sales skill development, such as negotiating or closing. They do this because they believe better execution of selling fundamentals will help to close business. Usually, this addresses a specific symptom, but not the systemic causes of the performance issue. Teaching sellers to close early, often, and aggressively, for example, without demonstrating value or understanding critical business issues will certainly lead to misalignment with Buyer 2.0.

- We've seen organizations invest in automated support tools for the sales team, such as CRM, knowledge management, and sales enablement applications, thinking these systems will improve efficiency and thus close performance gaps. CRM and related tools can be useful, but if they don't help with the sellers' effectiveness rather than simply their efficiency you may be in for a disaster. Think about it: if sellers are doing the wrong things and you improve their efficiency, you may only be helping them to do something bad or poorly more often.

In order to adapt successfully to the Buyer 2.0 paradigm, sales organizations need to recognize the larger trends, and then adjust how they engage with buyers on a more strategic level. There are three high-level aspects of the new buyer paradigm that, if thoughtfully considered, can help sales teams to successfully align with Buyer 2.0 norms:

1. Marketing and sales are blurring together.

2. Buyers are becoming highly informed comparison shoppers.

3. Risk aversion is the new normal.

Marketing and Sales Blur

The tenets of business development (sometimes known as stimulating interest or lead generation) within Solution Selling are still very relevant for marketing and sales today (i.e., don't lead with product; focus on critical business issues; focus on how you've helped others and on the results). The dilemma for sellers engaging with Buyer 2.0 is they are being forced out of the early interest stimulation or lead generation aspects of selling. However, our research shows that sellers who are involved earlier in the buying process, as opposed to reacting to an active lead, have a much higher probability of winning. The challenge for sellers, therefore, is how to engage early with Buyer 2.0 in a way that is not intrusive or disruptive to the buying process.

In addition, traditional marketing has less control over the perception of the company in the marketplace. With the emergence of blogging, discussion boards, improved search engine optimization, third-party information aggregation services, and social networks with communities (e.g., groups on LinkedIn), there are more conversations, opinions, experiences, and information about your organization and your products and services in cyberspace than ever.

However, while sellers and their organizations can no longer completely control the message, they can monitor, listen to, and participate in conversations and help to shape them.

Messaging and credibility building are no longer just the role of formal marketing departments. Many marketing organizations simply don't have the bandwidth to operate at levels this granular. To get back to the front of the buying process, sellers must now extensively engage in informal marketing: active participation in industry or community discussion groups to demonstrate thought leadership and credibility. They need to regularly engage in discussions that are taking place in relevant communities. To accomplish this, sellers need to become both literate and proficient in using social media. They need to become power users of new tools and technologies that allow them to engage efficiently when buyers are forming their initial ideas about a potential problem or emerging opportunity.

At the beginning of the purchase process, Buyer 2.0 is having conversations about possible alternatives, but not with sellers. However, sellers can find and participate in those conversations to help Buyer 2.0 understand and form a vision of a possible solution for the buyer's critical business issues. Sellers can influence and guide Buyer 2.0 in decisions to evaluate alternative solutions, by demonstrating they can contribute meaningfully to the conversation.

Buyer 2.0 Is a Comparison Shopper

Armed with an abundance of information resources, Buyer 2.0 is empowered to conduct extensive research and fact finding when suspecting a problem or need. More often than not, by the time an actual sales conversation takes place, Buyer 2.0 usually has a premise already forming about the nature of the problem and how to solve it. This doesn't mean the buyers are fully aware of the scope of their problems, the underlying reasons for them, or the financial impact to their business. It also doesn't mean they are objectively informed, but their perspective has already been shaped and influenced by a wide variety of resources and mediums.

This means a different level of sales conversation needs to occur. The seller needs to quickly ascertain where the buyer is in the buying process, the business drivers behind the buyer's interest, and the thoroughness of the buyer's premise or hypothesis for a potential solution. The ramifications here are clear: the seller must possess a high degree of *situational fluency* with respect to the buyer's industry, issues, best practices, and competitive pressures, as well as be able to objectively validate, enhance, or reengineer the perceptions of the buyer.

In addition, buyers may already have formed an opinion about the value a seller will bring to them if and when they decide to engage that seller. They may have searched on LinkedIn, Facebook, and other web-based media to formulate an opinion of individual sellers and their organizations.

During Buyer 2.0's research, it is important that sellers are seen in a favorable light—one that fosters credibility and also helps form, elevate, or confirm the seller's personal brand. This can be developed through participation in thought leadership conversations, authorship of relevant blog posts or white papers, associations that suggest professionalism in your job, and so forth. In essence, buyers are comparison shopping not only solutions, but also the people behind them.

Risk Aversion as the New Normal

Recent research indicates that nearly half of forecasted opportunities fail to close.[14] This is not the result of organizations failing to perceive problems they need to solve or failing to see opportunities they can capitalize on. There are other strategic factors that contribute to the high percentage of "failure to close" opportunities.

The global economic climate has undergone multiple forms of trauma in the past decade. The bursting of the Internet bubble was closely followed by events of 9/11, and the persistent instability of the global financial system has suppressed corporations' willingness to

---

[14]Jim Dickie, "2012 Sales Performance Optimization," *Sales Performance Optimization Report*, CSO Insights, Summer 2012. Accessed December 1, 2013.

invest. A by-product of this environment has been the emergence of increasingly sophisticated and powerful purchasing functions within corporations. These organizations have typically undergone extensive training in effective procurement and negotiation practices, and have created a new layer for sellers to navigate in order to succeed.

Buyer 2.0 is not just a more informed consumer, but also tends to involve an increasingly more risk-averse and sophisticated purchasing function. As a result, sellers in the Buyer 2.0 world will need to be exceptional in their abilities to position, articulate, and defend the value of their offerings. This is a key concept in dealing with Buyer 2.0. They must provide Buyer 2.0 with a compelling reason to act if there is not one naturally present. The financial impact, whether positive or negative and articulated in the form of the cost of delay, may be just the reason they need to take action.

Purchasing organizations are also arming themselves with formidable negotiating capabilities. In addition to increased levels of business acumen, sellers need to be well versed in principles of effective negotiation.

These higher levels of sales proficiency will require investment in both education and tools that integrate business acumen and value-based execution through the entire sales process. Sellers must be insightful and effective at legitimately helping the buyer rationalize the need to take action—in a manner that is mutually beneficial to both buying and selling parties.

The Relevancy of Solution Selling and the Evolution of the Collaborative Sale

At the beginning of this chapter, we posed the question of the continued relevancy of Solution Selling. The inherent design of this methodology, based on aligning with the buyer process, has enabled Solution Selling to remain useful and productive for sellers. The emergence of

Buyer 2.0 behavior, however, requires Solution Selling to adapt and evolve.

This evolution involves three distinct character parts—or more accurately, *personae*—that solution sellers must play in order to align with and engage successfully with Buyer 2.0: the Micro-Marketer, the Visualizer, and the Value Driver. These personae are each defined by a set of specific behaviors, competencies, and attitudes that enable sellers to succeed with today's buyers. By assuming the right selling persona at the right times, sellers can gain access to early-stage buyers and work in harmony with them throughout the entire evaluation and purchase decision process. We explore each of these personae in depth in Chapters 4, 5, and 6.

In addition, solution sellers must recognize the rise of Buyer 2.0 empowerment in the buying process. Sellers can no longer control buyers by dictating how and when they get access to information about solution alternatives. Instead, sellers need to recognize buyers as knowledgeable and empowered partners, and learn to collaborate effectively with them as a valued adviser and counselor. While Solution Selling historically stressed control over the buying process, the Collaborative Sale emphasizes more alignment and collaboration with Buyer 2.0 than control.

The Collaborative Sale enables sellers to:

- Engage with buyers when they are not seeking out sellers, without alienating and annoying them.

- Know where buyers are in their buying process and how to align with where they are (and not where a seller prefers them to be).

- Develop and demonstrate understanding about the buyer's industry, business trends, and best practices, and provide useful expertise and creative thinking.

- Create a vision of a solution, or capture and enhance the buyer's current vision, or reengineer the buyer's vision to new or better ways to solve problems or capitalize on opportunities.

- Capture and articulate the quantitative value of a solution in a way that is compelling for the buyer.

- Sell openly and transparently by sharing everything you know about the buyers' situations with them, so they know that you know.

- Bring new ideas, new products, and new services to the buyer even if they are not your own. This means always putting the buyer's interests first, before your own.

In summary, in order to do business with Buyer 2.0, sellers must collaborate with buyers as equals, focusing on solving the buyers' problems and providing value in every interaction throughout their buying process. In addition, sellers must learn how to play different parts (i.e., personae) within the customer's buying process, much like an actor might play different parts within a theatrical production.

The essential and foundational competency required for sellers to be effective with Buyer 2.0 is called *situational fluency*. This unique combination of knowledge, skills, abilities, and attitude is required of all collaborative sellers, and therefore is worthy of further examination, which we do in the next chapter.

The Story (Continued)

Nancy lowered her voice. "Jon, did you tell the broker anything about ExyRisk that he couldn't have researched on his own?"

"No, but people are busy. I didn't want to assume he'd done any research. I didn't want to just jump in, I wanted to warm him up and tell him what we're about."

"Jon, I advise three companies and they're telling me it's not uncommon for a C-suite exec to attend an initial meeting with a vendor. Even if they're not C-suite guys, buyers have been coached by supply chain experts to do their homework before appointments. The fact that you got a warm introduction put you ahead, but you didn't maximize that lift."

She lowered her voice even further, "Customers respect sellers who are smart, who know about their business, understand their problems and can give them ideas, first and foremost. That's the value you're offering, far more than the product. *You* are the value, through what you know and what you've helped others achieve."

Nancy leaned across the table to look Jon straight in the eye, "Now I know you're accustomed to doing demos early in the sales process, so you'll be surprised when I tell you that the demo isn't the best next step."

Jon sat up, ramrod straight. "You're kidding."

"From where I sit, the most successful salespeople hold product back until they're convinced they can provide real value. What about your insurance broker? What has your prospect told you about his revenue shortfalls?"

"Nothing, but who doesn't need more revenue?"

"How are you going to get your foot back in the door with him?"

"I've been trying to figure that out."

They both leaned back in their chairs. Nancy said nothing as Jon chewed the inside of his cheek, deep in thought.

"You know, I got that appointment through a friend who sold his interests in the brokerage when he retired. He's been gone a few years, but thought there was a place for ExyRisk, especially with what new technologies are able to do to forecast and analyze wacky weather. He called ahead and I got the appointment."

Nancy said, "All's not lost. You struck out on the first meeting, but on the strength of your referral you can probably get one more appointment with him if you show him that you've done some work and have something to offer besides a demo. Let's get to work."

3 What the New Buyers Expect: Situational Fluency

Psychologists define a *persona* as a social role or a character played by an actor. The word is derived from Latin, where it originally referred to a theatrical mask.[1] In *The Collaborative Sale* we are introducing you to three new sales personae, which are character parts that sellers must play within the buyer's process in order to be successful with Buyer 2.0.

So what does this mean, exactly? It means that no matter what job title, function, or role a seller may take on, the seller must assume the mask or the persona that selling to Buyer 2.0 requires.

We want to be perfectly clear about what we are saying. To help us do this, let's first take a look at how sellers are often categorized. For example, sellers can be classified by different types, profiles, roles, or titles. Figure 3.1 displays only a few of the dozens of different classifications of sellers that we've seen our clients use.

---

[1]Paul Bishop, "Conclusion: The Development of the Personality," Chapter 5 in *Analytical Psychology and German Classical Aesthetics: Goethe, Schiller and Jung* (London: Routledge, 2008), 157–158.

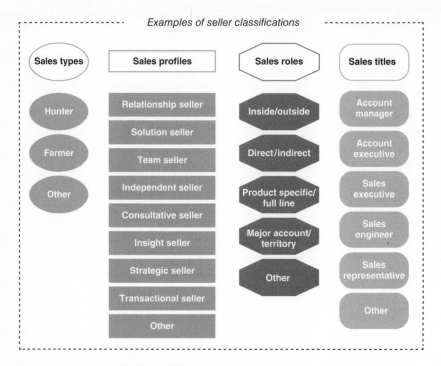

Figure 3.1   Examples of Seller Classifications

Another example of seller classification is used by the Chally Group, which provides a hierarchical model of sales roles organized into 12 different selling job functions, classified by hunter/farmer, inside/outside, direct/indirect, specialized product/full line, and major account/territory. (See Figure 3.2.)[2]

A persona is not a sales title, type, profile, or job role. A persona is a character role that sellers need to assume and play no matter how they are categorized or profiled, in order to be successful with Buyer 2.0. For example, some sellers prefer to pursue new business in new accounts—they are often called hunters. Other sellers prefer to cultivate relationships and grow recurring business with existing

---

[2]Howard Stevens, "How to Select a Sales Force That Sells," *Executive Briefs*, Chally Group, July 2012. Accessed December 1, 2013, at http://chally.com/executive-briefings/.

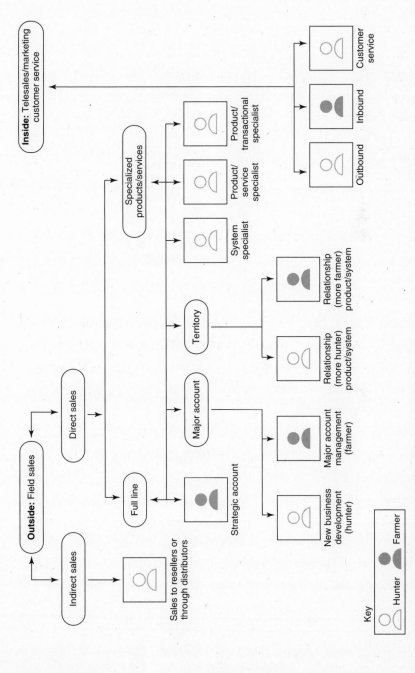

Figure 3.2 Chally Group Sales Job Classifications

41

accounts—they are typically called farmers. Both are legitimate and valuable sales types. Both are useful, but with a different focus. Both can achieve high levels of success with Buyer 2.0 if they assume the correct persona at the right time, in order to align with the buyer's process and state of mind. No matter the sellers' type, role, or function, they must assume the right character parts as they interact with Buyer 2.0. All three personae in *The Collaborative Sale*—the Micro-Marketer, the Visualizer, and the Value Driver—are usually played in every sales opportunity involving Buyer 2.0.

Seller Agility

A collaborative seller must know when to play the right persona, in order to keep in harmony with Buyer 2.0. There is not a single best or only sales persona that always produces the highest results. Instead, the most effective selling persona is the one that matches each specific customer situation and aligns with Buyer 2.0's current state. An effective seller knows how to play all three sales personae and can migrate easily between them, from one to another as needed. This is called *seller agility*.

Analyzing what individual sellers need in order to play each persona successfully reveals the essential competencies required for each. This can be very useful for evaluating the suitability of candidates for certain selling jobs, or for determining what knowledge, skills, and abilities need to be developed for executing the sales personae and for higher levels of performance. Sellers who lack the right competencies or the necessary sales agility to execute all types of sales personae are more likely to fail because they cannot adjust and align with Buyer 2.0.

The three sales personae of *The Collaborative Sale* align with Buyer 2.0's concerns as they progress through the buying process. In actual practice, the application of the three sales personae overlaps.

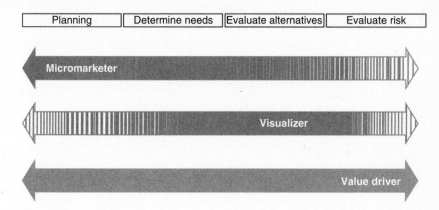

Figure 3.3 Sales Personae in the Buying Process

(See Figure 3.3.) Each can be utilized at any point of the buying process, as required.

- The *Micro-Marketer persona* is typically played by sellers when engaging with Buyer 2.0 early in the buying process. This persona seeks to provide useful advice and innovative ideas to potential buyers who are in the latent stage of their buying process when the goal is to stimulate their interest or to help shape their view of possible solutions. However, the Micro-Marketer persona really never ends. Sellers continuously need to create and stimulate demand as well as grow their pipelines with new opportunities, without exception.

- The *Visualizer persona* is typically played in the middle of Buyer 2.0's buying process. The Visualizer seeks to create, expand, or reengineer visions of solutions that are compelling, so the buyer wants to take action. Being able to collaborate with buyers, understand their situations, and provide valuable insight and visions on how to address their issues are key Visualizer competencies.

- The *Value Driver persona* is played by sellers throughout Buyer 2.0's entire buying process. The Value Driver never stops thinking about value. This persona literally leads with, sells with, and closes with the value of the solution. Value Drivers give buyers a compelling reason to act and avoid the negative impact of delay, and they use value to mitigate buyer perceptions of risk.

The foundational competency required for mastery of all three of the personae in *The Collaborative Sale* is called *situational fluency*.

Situational Fluency

Conversations between buyers and sellers have to change. As we learned in the previous chapter, the profound changes in buyer behavior dictate this. The sales conversation can no longer focus on the seller's products and services; it must be about the buyer's business results. Buyer 2.0 specifically wants to talk and do business with sellers who understand buyers' business, situations, challenges, and opportunities. They have very little time for a generalist. They prefer to deal with a specialist in their given field or industry.

Buyer 2.0 does not have time for overly aggressive or excessively friendly sellers who are only interested in selling them something. After all, Buyer 2.0's process isn't about the seller at all. Buyer 2.0 wants sellers to collaborate with them, to act more like consultants, and to provide useful expertise.

This requires sellers to possess a foundational selling competency called *situational fluency*. It is a unique combination of knowledge, skills, abilities, and attitude that makes sellers effective with today's buyers. It is the key competency required to execute successfully all three personae of the Collaborative Sale.

Ironically, we have found that many sales managers tend to look for certain qualities when hiring sellers, but those qualities are often different from what most buyers want and look for in sellers.

Sales managers tend to seek sellers with successful track records and great selling skills—someone who can close business. Buyers, in contrast, want to engage with someone who really knows their business and who is interested in helping them solve problems and achieve results. However, this doesn't mean these two very different desires have to be mutually exclusive. With good situational fluency, sellers can do both—they can help buyers solve problems while at the same time helping their own organization reach sales and revenue targets.

So, why don't companies simply change their hiring and development practices to align with what buyers want in sellers? It is really very simple: they are too short-term focused. Organizations depend upon monthly and quarterly results, and they think assertive or aggressive sellers who push for the business are the answer. In truth, this is really very old-fashioned thinking.

Granted, previous sales success and some assertiveness are useful characteristics in selling, but they don't ensure future success. This is particularly true when selling into new industries, or selling new products and services, or selling under a new business model. For example, take our story about Jon in our opening chapter. His past success was due in large part to selling in periods of high demand when winning business was much easier than it is today. High-demand markets are like rising tides—they help to float all boats.

Components of Situational Fluency

As illustrated in Figure 3.4, the three components of situational fluency are:

1. *Knowledge*—situational knowledge and capability knowledge
2. *Skills*—people skills and selling skills
3. *Attitude*—willingness to collaborate

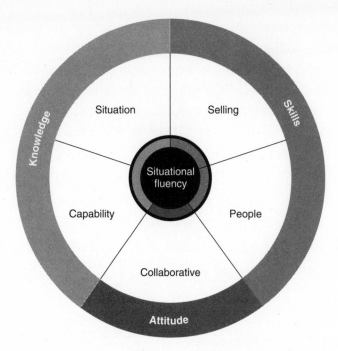

Figure 3.4   Components of Situational Fluency

Situational Knowledge

Knowledge is both the awareness of something, as well as any
information, understanding, or skill one learns from experience
or education. Situational knowledge is the awareness of a buyer's
circumstances, as well as the understanding of the implications of
that situation based on the seller's experience or learning. A thorough
knowledge and understanding of the buyer's industry, trends, key
players, problems, challenges, opportunities, and desired results is
therefore a requirement for sellers today. Remember, Buyer 2.0 wants
to do business with sellers who can collaborate with buyers to help
them see ways of solving problems, including those they may have
not yet seen or considered. How can a seller do this without first
understanding the buyer's situation and what it means?

Buyer 2.0 doesn't have time to spend on sellers who only pitch products or services, especially when what they pitch isn't a capability that is relevant or it doesn't solve a problem. Sellers who don't understand the buyer's business are reduced in status to mere vendors, not the valued and trusted advisers they aspire and need to be.

Capability Knowledge

Sellers must know more than just the essential capabilities of their products or services; they must also know how those capabilities can be converted into a desired result. Sellers' capability knowledge enables them to collaborate and create visions of possible solutions for buyers.

When Buyer 2.0 engages sellers, the sellers are expected to add value immediately. Therefore, sellers must not only understand their own products or services and the capabilities they can provide, but they must also have very good knowledge of available alternatives in the marketplace that could address the buyer's challenges or opportunities.

One caution: too often, product and services training focuses on features and functions, bells and whistles, or "speeds and feeds," and not enough on applications and results. Collaborative sellers need to know what their capabilities *do* for customers, and not just what the capabilities *are*.

People Skills

Though they are universally acknowledged as vital to the success of sellers, interpersonal or people skills have many different definitions and descriptions.

In 1936, Dale Carnegie popularized the value of people skills in his book *How to Win Friends and Influence People*.[3] In the original 1936

---

[3] Dale Carnegie, *How to Win Friends and Influence People* (New York: Simon & Schuster, 1936; rev. ed. 1981).

edition, he described the power of interpersonal skills for sellers, saying that they "Enable you to win new clients, [and] new customers.... Increase your earning power.... Make you a better salesman."[4]

According to Harriet Rifkin of the *Business Journal News Service*, "people skills" are described as:

- Understanding ourselves and moderating our responses
- Talking effectively and empathizing accurately
- Building relationships of trust, respect, and productive interactions[5]

The *Macmillan Dictionary* provides a more succinct definition of people skills: "The ability to communicate effectively with people in a friendly way, especially in business."[6]

Our clients have shared various ways of describing people skills with us. Some of the typical characteristics of individuals with good people skills are:

- They understand themselves and how their behavior impacts others.
- They control their responses; they try to be less impulsive and to think before acting.
- They have a sincere desire to assist others in the pursuit of goals; they are able to tune in accurately to the feelings and needs of others and then treat people accordingly.

---

[4]"How to Win Friends and Influence People," *Wikipedia*, Wikimedia Foundation, August 12, 2013. Accessed December 1, 2013, at http://en.wikipedia.org/wiki/How_to_Win_Friends_and_Influence_People.

[5]Harriet Rifkin, "Invest in People Skills to Boost Bottom Line," *Portland Business Journal*, June 2, 2002. Accessed December 1, 2013, at www.bizjournals.com/portland/stories/2002/06/03/focus6.html.

[6]"People Skills," definition by *Macmillan Dictionary* (Basingstoke, UK: Macmillan Publishers Limited, 2009). Accessed December 1, 2013, at www.macmillandictionary.com/dictionary/british/people-skills.

- They work at managing relationships, building networks, and finding common ground in order to minimize conflict and maximize rapport.
- They are consistently approachable.
- They create an environment of trust.

People buy from people, and they are much more likely to buy from people whom they like. More importantly in this risk-averse world, people are very hesitant to collaborate with people they dislike. Therefore, the collaborative seller must possess good people skills, no matter whether engaging with buyers face-to-face or by any other means. But collaborative sellers must be more than just likable experts. They must get customers excited about a new solution, appealing to Buyer 2.0's emotions as well as intellect.

Selling Skills

At their most basic level, the skills required to sell are learned abilities that allow people to carry out specific tasks that lead to predetermined results within a specified period of time. Quite simply, selling skills are taught and learned—they are not something you are born with. This is contrary to many people's beliefs who say, "He or she is a natural-born seller." Sellers are not born; they are developed.

This does not mean that certain human characteristics associated with sellers, such as being friendly, persuasive, talkative, outgoing, and likable, are not characteristics that many good sellers have. In fact, they often do have these qualities. The key point is these characteristics alone do not make a good seller.

Selling skills are those that allow the successful execution of specific selling activities, including but not limited to stimulating interest, qualifying opportunities, determining needs, diagnosing problems, presenting, negotiating, and closing, to cite some common examples. The skills required for these selling activities—often called sales competencies—can be developed to higher levels of mastery and proficiency with training, practice, and coaching. Sellers who commit themselves to continuous learning and improvement of these skills are better equipped to engage effectively with Buyer 2.0.

Collaborative Attitude

Collaborating with Buyer 2.0 requires more than just skills and knowledge; it also requires the right attitude. Sellers must be willing to work with buyers in a spirit of openness and transparency. Collaborative sellers share and explain the reasons for their methods and approaches openly with buyers, and they consistently demonstrate that they are acting with the buyer's interests in mind first.

This attitude represents a much different outlook for most sellers. A product-focused seller considers success to be a sale, even if that means a less than optimal outcome for the buyer. A collaborative seller starts with a mind-set that the buyer's interests are of paramount importance, even if that means qualifying out of a sale. The key is to always act in the best interests of the buyer, even if that means a smaller sale or no sale at all. Buyer 2.0 values sellers who do the right thing, especially if the buyer knows the actions a seller takes are not in the seller's sole interest, but in the buyer's own best interests. In the long run, these are the sellers that earn lasting trust, loyalty, and repeat business from buyers.

The five components of situational fluency—situational knowledge, capability knowledge, people skills, selling skills, and collaborative attitude—are all required when selling to Buyer 2.0.

Hiring for Situational Fluency

As we mentioned earlier, sales managers tend to hire sellers who exhibit good people and selling skills, before any other considerations.

They generally seek people who show they are strong closers of business, with good track records of achieving or exceeding their assigned sales goals.

Although past success can be a useful indicator of future performance, it is no guarantee, especially when selling to Buyer 2.0, who wants consultative sellers who add value to the buying process, insightfully diagnose buyers' situations, and prescribe the specific capabilities that will help them reach or exceed their goals. Sales managers should therefore look for people who exhibit all five aspects of situational fluency, or who demonstrate a willingness to develop the required components of situational fluency quickly. If a sales manager ignores any of the five components of situational fluency in evaluating candidates for sales positions, it will likely result in hiring people who cannot collaborate with and sell to Buyer 2.0.

We suggest that companies conduct and or use assessment vehicles to assist them during the hiring process to determine the candidate's situational fluency. We describe these kinds of assessments in more detail in Chapter 9.

Developing Situational Fluency

An important question for sales executives is: can situational fluency be developed quickly, or is it learned only through time and direct experience? In working with clients, we have discovered that it can be developed to high levels of proficiency quickly with a combination of training, reinforcement, and coaching.

If your company provides only product training for sellers, don't be surprised when sellers fail. When the emphasis of training is on details of products and services to be sold instead of about the problems and opportunities they address within a customer's business or situation, it is almost impossible for sellers to develop sufficient situational fluency. There must be a balance of training and development for situational knowledge and capability knowledge, with practice and coaching for selling skills and people skills. We have also found that when sellers are suitably equipped with the right knowledge and skills, they tend to develop the right collaborative attitude as well, especially when it is reinforced with consistent messaging from their managers.

Training for Situational Fluency

SiriusDecisions is an industry research firm that examines best practices in sales and marketing. It conducts in-depth research studies on what makes sellers effective. Jim Ninivaggi, Service Director of Sales Enablement Strategies at SiriusDecisions, shared some of its recent findings on training and onboarding of sales professionals with us:

"At our client forums and roundtable discussions, sales managers confessed that they had lost their focus on the importance of the human trust factor for the past few years when they designed their sales training and onboarding programs. Most of them basically give salespeople a week of training—sitting through presentation after presentation—and then the salespeople are thrown out into the field, and their managers are told that they have to develop them. This produces a vicious cycle of lost productivity, not to mention frustrated new reps and sales managers.

"I say: don't make new hires practice their skills on buyers first! Everything should be taught, practiced, and coached, from the way they open calls to the insights they share, the case studies they highlight, and how they make suggestions to buyers. Salespeople are clamoring for this kind of training, and smart companies are getting back to these basics.

"We see that buyers are inundated with data, so they want sellers to make it easy to do business with them. Properly trained salespeople make it easy for buyers to understand how their solutions are differentiated and how those resources can be leveraged for success."[7]

Technology's Role in Situational Fluency

For many sellers, situational knowledge is more difficult to develop than capability knowledge. Fortunately, technology now provides opportunities for sellers to develop situational knowledge more quickly. Tracking relevant industry trends and events is much easier today using tools like Google Alerts, InsideView, web content aggregation sites, Twitter Search, LinkedIn discussion groups, OneSource iSell trigger event monitoring, and many other applications.

These sales enablement tools can help sellers to follow key accounts' website changes, tweets from buyers, and related blogs. They can help to identify key players and individuals to target, connect with, and join in online discussions. They can make it easier to follow industry analysts and monitor relevant business trends of interest to buyers. By tracking job postings, keeping up with financial trends, and setting up automated keyword tracking agents on targeted companies, sellers can identify business issues worthy of further investigation and possible development into a sales opportunity. Finally, automated tools can help sellers to monitor the activities of direct competitors and to learn more about their capabilities.

Automated monitoring of customers' businesses and relevant industry trends takes some time to set up, but once in place, it can

---

[7]SPI telephone interview with Jim Ninivaggi, SiriusDecisions, October 17, 2013.

provide a well-tuned stream of relevant information that will help sellers to develop proficiency in understanding their customer situations and how to address them. This can help sellers to develop higher levels of situational fluency faster.

Developing Situational Fluency at PNC Bank

PNC Bank, headquartered in Pittsburgh, Pennsylvania, offers a wide range of banking services for customers, from individuals and small businesses to corporations and government entities. Getting to know the bankers at PNC Bank has been a pleasure, and we are very impressed with their commitment to their customers and their employees.

PNC Bank teaches commercial relationship bankers, who manage portfolios of diverse industries, to integrate research into their precall planning in order to develop their situational fluency. We recently sat down with Senior Vice President and Market Leader Robert "Bobby" Chesney from Charlotte, North Carolina, and asked him about the importance of developing situational fluency.

"Our goal is to provide the customers with the value they would normally receive from us in the second call or second conversation but accomplish this in our first call or meeting with them. In order for this to happen, we've paid for industry data that a relationship manager has access to and can easily grasp before calling on a customer.

"For example, a banker calling on a manufacturer can become familiar with innovative processing equipment that has just been introduced to the market. Armed with research, he

might say, for example, 'There are 27 manufacturing companies in our region. I'd like to share with you what similar
manufacturers of your size are doing.'

"The banker will go on to talk about the value and ROI [return
on investment] on the new equipment that could help the
company compete. The bankers' research and planning process
helps develop their situational fluency and prepares them for
this conversation in advance. We know that our bankers add
value because they have done their research beforehand."[8]

---

[8] SPI personal interview with Robert Chesney, PNC Bank, October 23, 2013.

Part II
Three
Personae of
the Collaborative
Sale

4 The Micro-Marketer Persona

Numerous studies cited previously in this book show that buyers may complete over half of their purchase evaluation process *before* contacting a potential seller. (See Figure 4.1.) Since buyers now prefer to conduct initial research and needs evaluation on their own before contacting potential solution providers, should sellers attempt to engage with buyers early in their buying process? And if so, can sellers do so without annoying or alienating them?

Our research and experience with clients shows that even though Buyer 2.0 now waits longer to invite sellers to participate, there are still effective ways that sellers can engage with early-stage buyers—either before or just as buyers are beginning to think about a possible purchase. Better yet, sellers can engage early in ways that Buyer 2.0 finds both valuable and appreciated. In fact, our clients report that when their sellers engage first with a buyer, they win business over *five times more often* than other sellers who wait for buyers to engage them.

There is a right way to gain access to and influence early-stage buyers, but it means significant changes in how most sellers conduct business development. To find new opportunities with Buyer 2.0, sellers must embrace and master a new persona—the Micro-Marketer.

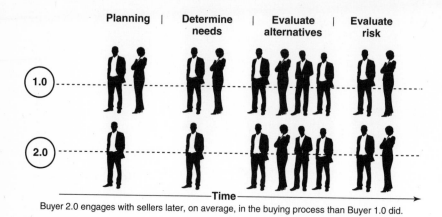

Buyer 2.0 engages with sellers later, on average, in the buying process than Buyer 1.0 did.

Figure 4.1   Buyer 1.0 versus Buyer 2.0 Engagement of Sellers

The Micro-Marketer persona enables a seller to connect with and converse with early-stage buyers, demonstrate the credibility and value of a personal brand, and influence buyers' understanding about potential solutions to problems or about potential opportunities for improved results.

Why Be a Micro-Marketer?

Historically, it has been the marketing department's job to influence market perceptions, demonstrate thought leadership, stimulate buyer interest, and generate leads. The sales department was responsible for turning those leads into closed business. This traditional division of labor, and the mutual understanding of the interdepartmental hand-off, was clear.

However, when we poll our clients, they tell us that they cannot depend solely on their marketing departments to provide all the leads they need to achieve their assigned goals. The reason is because most marketing departments, which tend to look at markets strategically, do not know the specifics of individual buyers, accounts, and territories as well as sellers who are serving those assignments.

A 2012 research study by CSO Insights[1] corroborates our findings. That study showed that marketing departments provide a little more than one-third of qualified sales leads pursued by sellers. This means that most new prospects had to be discovered through sellers' own efforts, which is probably why the same study showed that about 60 percent of marketing organizations rated themselves as "needing improvement" in providing the right quality and quantity of leads to their sales teams.

For a seller, the Micro-Marketer persona means becoming a "marketing department of one" for engaging with early-stage buyers and stimulating the interest of prospects in a targeted territory or in an account, or who are individual buyers. It means developing a mind-set where sellers take personal responsibility for generating their own potential business.

The kind of business development activities that effective sellers perform is changing. Sellers need to engage in an effective mix of targeted marketing activities, which may include telephone canvassing, e-mail distributions, online and in-person seminars, direct mail, trade shows, industry associations, and related events to find prospects. In addition, sellers also need to find where their buyers are having online conversations, and participate in them.

In the world of the social web, the new buyers can participate easily in online conversations about their goals and aspirations with like-minded people. It is simple for them to find others with whom they share much in common by joining topic-specific interest groups such as those found on LinkedIn, or through other social media sites and industry forums. By joining these online resources, they can talk with peers who understand their challenges and who can exchange useful ideas.

---

[1] *Sales Performance Optimization Report*, CSO Insights, 2012. Also at www.csoinsights.com.

Therefore, sellers must recognize that Buyer 2.0 is having conversations all the time about the kinds of capabilities that sellers can provide. Sellers must also understand they cannot simply insert themselves into the middle of those conversations using traditional broadcast marketing techniques. They must know how to engage effectively in online social discussions.

Micro-Marketers Demonstrate Situational Fluency—With Constraint

Let us be perfectly clear. The Micro-Marketer persona is not about a seller broadcasting generalized messages. It is about collaborating with deliberately selected buyers about specific issues that are of importance to them.

Sellers who master the persona of Micro-Marketer act differently than the usual salesperson. They do *not* try to sell overtly when first interacting with Buyer 2.0 in online conversations and during business development activities early in the buying process. Instead, they focus on contributing relevant insights to those conversations. They share pertinent ideas and observations from their own expertise and experience. By providing useful information and answering questions that may arise, Micro-Marketers have the opportunity to position themselves as useful *thought leaders*, or experts in their field of specialization.

Sellers must be very careful in how they communicate with Buyer 2.0 early in a potential buying cycle. If the buyers get any hint of a seller being pushy or aggressive, they will ignore *or even block* the seller from the conversation. If they think that a seller is pressing ahead with an idea or agenda that is not in their interests or is not relevant to their situation, they may shut out the seller from the conversation. In fact, if Buyer 2.0 perceives that the seller is just trying to *sell something*, instead of contributing expertise and informed perspectives to the conversation, the buyers will almost always stop participation in further discussion with that seller.

Dave Stein, founder and CEO of ES Research Group, and who wrote the Foreword to this book, observed that it is counterintuitive for most sellers to restrain themselves in early engagement with buyers. "They'd rather do mass market appeals, hoping something sticks that they can drive to a sale," he says. He believes that the early part of the sale is "where a seller can be a worthy collaborator to a knowledgeable buyer, and showing knowledge and thought leadership is foundational to that collaboration."[2]

Many sellers are reluctant to position themselves as experts, especially if they are new to their positions. They lack the confidence in their own knowledge to consider themselves an authority. However, many of these sellers are shortchanging themselves—they are more knowledgeable than they think. They simply don't yet realize how they can provide specific expertise in a useful way to Buyer 2.0.

As we explained in the previous chapter, the most important competency for the Micro-Marketer is *situational fluency*. In order to become confident about their own expertise, sellers must cultivate relevant knowledge about customers' situations, industry trends, best practices, and business drivers. In addition, they must be able to articulate their understanding clearly and in a compelling way. Most of all, they must be able to provide a perspective that helps Buyer 2.0 to visualize their world in a new way.

Micro-Marketers Create Their Own Personal Brand

The best Micro-Marketers not only represent their organization's capabilities, but they are also able to provide their own unique, individual

---

[2]SPI telephone interview with Dave Stein, ES Research Group, October 1, 2013.

brand to customers. They work continuously to develop their expertise and to diligently convey their value to buyers as a *personal brand*.

A brand is what identifies one seller's unique abilities distinctly from other alternatives. People evaluate alternative brands in their buying choices all the time. They consider Coca-Cola versus Pepsi, Acura versus Lexus, McDonald's versus Burger King, or Apple versus Microsoft when evaluating the kinds of products or services that each brand represents. There is safety and reassurance in selecting a strong brand, because it represents a consistent ability to deliver on a set of buyer expectations and perceptions. Buyers know, or at least they think that they know, what they are getting when they buy a well-established brand.

Whether sellers are consciously aware of it or not, they are creating their personal brand through their actions. A seller's brand is his or her reputation—what the seller is personally known for. Jeff Bezos, founder of Amazon.com, once said, "Your brand is what people say about you when you're not in the room."[3] A seller's personal brand is completely separate from the organization they represent.

Sellers who assume the Micro-Marketer persona recognize the importance of their personal brand. They actively develop their personal brand to differentiate themselves, so that buyers perceive them as credible, trustworthy, expert, and a distinct value-add, especially when compared to other alternatives.

To define their personal brand, sellers should first consider some introspective questions, such as, "What is it about me that makes me unique? What have I accomplished that I can share with others? What do I want to be remembered by?" Sellers can evaluate what they think their brand is today, and then examine whether there is a gap between that and where they want to be.

---

[3]Kate T. May, "10 Brand Stories from Tim Leberecht's TED Talk," *TED Blog*, TED, October 8, 2012. Accessed December 1, 2013, at http://blog.ted.com/2012/10/08/10-brand-stories-from-tim-leberechts-tedtalk/.

Sellers can then compose a personal brand statement—a promise made to themselves and to their customers. It should be a simple statement that summarizes their core values and beliefs and makes that seller stand out. It should be authentic and true to who they think they are. This brand statement should be simple (easy to remember and communicate to others), relevant (they can connect it to what they do), and believable (because seller credibility depends on it).

With a clear personal brand statement, sellers can then build their reputation by becoming better known in the world they service—their industry, accounts, customers, and potential buyers. They can begin to increase visibility of their personal brand in that world.

Gary Vaynerchuk, author of the *New York Times* best seller *Crush It!*, said, "I think that it is important to build a personal brand.... Your reputation online and in the new business world is pretty much the game, and so you've got to be a good person because you can't hide anything and more importantly, you've got to be out there at some level."[4]

It is in sellers' best interests to consider how their personal brand is perceived online and to take steps to improve it on an ongoing basis. Micro-Marketers can monitor the development of their online personal brand, using tools like Klout and Peer Index, which track the extent and effectiveness of their developing presence on the social web. Other sites like BrandYourself.com and Reputation.com further help sellers improve their chances to be found online—and also to appear in a positive light.

Jill Rowley is an example of someone who has developed a personal brand. Rowley leveraged social media to become one of the top sales representatives for Eloqua, a leading marketing automation platform. As the self-proclaimed "Eloqueen," Rowley used tools like

---

[4]Gary Vaynerchuk, "Building a Personal Brand: It's Your Only Option," *Big Think Blog*, Big Think, August 26, 2013. Accessed December 11, 2013, at http://bigthink.com/videos/building-a-personal-brand-its-your-only-option.

blogs, LinkedIn, Twitter, and Facebook to "socially surround" her prospects and add value long before any sales engagement took place. When Oracle acquired Eloqua in 2012, they hired Rowley to further the cause of what is now called Social Selling at Oracle, with the appropriate title of Social Selling Evangelist.

"The modern sales professional is actually not a seller, but is someone who helps people buy," Rowley says. "This is someone who helps the buyer understand his problem, helps the buyer understand there's a solution to the problem, and helps the buyer understand why her company is uniquely qualified to solve the buyer's problem. Today's buyers are better informed by information available via the web and social connections."[5]

By establishing a persistent online presence and using this to demonstrate expertise and thought leadership, Micro-Marketers can convey their personal brand to Buyer 2.0, and also help shape the buyer's initial vision of potential solutions to problems before any further sales engagement. By becoming a valued contributor to the conversation with Buyer 2.0, sellers can once again connect with prospective customers early in their buying process—and in so doing, they can influence the requirements and specifications required in eventual purchases.

Planning and Executing a Micro-Marketer Strategy

Once sellers have developed relevant situational fluency and defined their personal brand, they can then plan and execute a Micro-Marketer

---

[5] Jill Rowley, "The ABCs of Social Selling: Always Be Connected," *It's All about Revenue: The Revenue Marketing Blog*, Oracle/Eloqua, February 27, 2013. Accessed December 11, 2013, at http://blog.eloqua.com/abcssocialselling/.

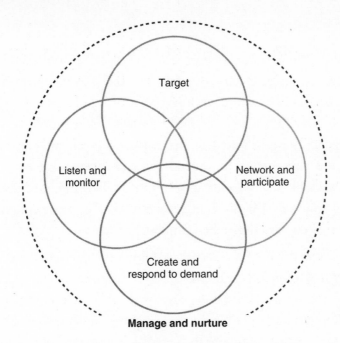

Figure 4.2 Components of Micro-Marketer Strategy

strategy. The five components of a Micro-Marketer strategy, illustrated in Figure 4.2, are:

1. *Target.* Identify the key audiences to focus Micro-Marketer activity upon.

2. *Listen and monitor.* Identify and track the most relevant resources for buyer conversations.

3. *Network and participate.* Connect with buyers and contribute to conversations.

4. *Create and respond to demand.* Cultivate any stimulated or expressed interest of buyers.

5. *Manage and nurture.* Maintain connection and provide value to latent buyers.

Target

In order to stimulate the interest of Buyer 2.0, sellers must first decide *what kinds* of buyers they need to interest. This may sound obvious, but few sellers take the time to think about the ideal kinds of problems that their capabilities can solve, and who owns those problems—that is, the specific jobs, in specific industries and departmental functions, that are held accountable for the business and performance issues that a seller's capabilities could address or improve. These key buyer roles are the ideal targets for Micro-Marketer activities. They represent the most likely prospects with the highest potential for buying.

Once the ideal target criteria have been established, sellers can then narrow the scope of where they can find those potential buyers. What online social groups would they participate in? What industry or trade association resources would they find valuable? What specific companies and individuals represent the best fit with the target criteria? Do those companies maintain their own blogs and online forums? Sellers can use the target criteria to determine where they can find Buyer 2.0 conversations—and where they need to listen and monitor.

Listen and Monitor

Sellers can subscribe to RSS feeds on relevant customer and industry websites to receive regular updates and bulletins. They can establish keyword searches using tools like Google Alerts, Twitter Search, and Social Mention.

They may also set up trigger event monitors in tools such as InsideeView, Nimble, and SalesLoft to keep a finger on the pulse of the latest trends and news that would be of interest to their buyers. For example, sellers could set the search term *declining sales revenue* in InsideView for designated accounts or industries, if that is relevant to their capabilities, and then periodically scan all related notifications sent to their e-mail inbox to see if any articles indicate a potential opportunity.

We recommend that sellers who are new to online communities approach them quietly at first. Observe the kind of questions that are being asked, the discussions that generate the most controversy, the resources that are most frequently shared and quoted, and the manner in which people who overstep the social norms of the community are treated. This kind of quiet observation is often referred to as "lurking," a term that sounds more sinister than it really is. Lurkers watch others in an online community without actively participating, and doing this initially helps sellers to learn the community's accepted code of conduct.

We've heard sad tales about sellers who violated acceptable online community behavior, where they lost valuable social capital with potential buyers and current customers. No one wants to do business with someone who does not comply with behavioral norms, and it's easy to get that reputation if you aren't aware of the expected social conventions used in online social groups. When in doubt, find and ask one of the founders or current administrators of the group, forum, blog, or website. Usually, they are happy to provide any formal guidelines or recommended dos and don'ts for engaging with other participants or group members.

By listening and monitoring, sellers can be alerted to situations that may be ideal for subsequent engagement in direct demand-creation activities, using relevant messaging that references the alert source. For example, after reading an alert about an event in a target financial services company, a seller may send a message to an identified potential buyer, beginning with: "John, I recently read an article on XYZ online news detailing your recent acquisition and merger, and the impact that was likely to have on revenue attainment. We have helped other financial services organizations surpass revenue targets during major acquisitions...." This personalized message is more relevant to the buyer, and is more likely to be received and acted upon.

Network and Participate

Another important component of a Micro-Marketer strategy is to network and participate. Since Buyer 2.0 is using the social web to conduct their own research and interact with peers to discuss problems and solutions, sellers need to find those conversations, contribute to them, and be of genuine help and value, if they can. Once again, specific targeting criteria can help to identify the most relevant online resources and groups to join. These may include Facebook pages, Google+ communities, LinkedIn groups, and trade association and industry forums. An increasing number of companies themselves also host public blogs and forums, and sellers should routinely review any provided by targeted prospects.

Targeted prospect individuals may have their own blogs, Twitter accounts, LinkedIn profiles and groups, and Facebook pages. By using LinkedIn, for example, sellers can review useful information about the identified contact's background, education, specialties, and employment history, as well as social web groups where the contact may participate. They can also see if they share common connections, which they might use to get further advice or insight, or to gain a warm introduction. Twitter Search can also help sellers gain further insight about the contact and the industry.

To build their personal brands, the best Micro-Marketers work diligently to develop their own online presence. In addition to monitoring and participating in social web activities, some also start their own blogs and post to them regularly, or they use approved blogging resources provided by their organizations.

Using a "microblog" service like Twitter to distribute links to relevant news stories, or to links to the seller's blog posts about the implications of such developments and what they could mean to buyers, can be of profound interest to a seller's intended audience. Some sellers use automated content-gathering technology, like Curata, Scoop.it, and Paper.li, to assemble useful websites for targeted buyers,

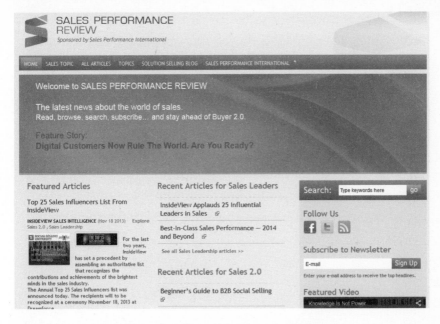

Figure 4.3   Example of a Curated Content Website

which coincidentally help them to remain abreast of current business trends. (See Figure 4.3 for an example of a curated website —in this case, SPI's *Sales Performance Review* page at www .salesperformancereview.com, which uses Curata to collect information about sales performance improvement for our clients.)

By setting up information distribution processes with a service such as Buffer or Twitterfeed, and by consolidating online updates using a tool such as HootSuite or Sprout Social, Micro-Marketers can post simultaneously to Twitter and other online social networking sites with minimal effort, providing convenient links to useful news items of interest to buyers.

Create and Respond to Demand

As sellers network and participate in social web conversations, they will discover buyer situations that represent ideal opportunities for solving problems and creating new value. This is when sellers should follow up directly and attempt to create buyer interest in how they might help their specific situation. This must be done tactfully and in the context of the conversation, in order to be effective.

For example, in response to a recent exchange of ideas on an industry forum, a seller might send a message starting with: "John, I'm glad you found my response to your question in the Mergers & Acquisitions Group on LinkedIn to be helpful. I have been thinking about your challenge, and I wanted personally follow up with you...." The seller can then outline some potential ideas, and recommended next steps.

Nurture and Manage

Even if executing the Micro-Marketer persona does not result in immediate sales opportunities, it serves another important purpose: it enables faster and more proficient development of situational fluency in a seller. As they hear relevant news and trends, sellers become more knowledgeable about their buyers' industry, businesses, and best practices. As they build their expertise, sellers will develop greater confidence and more insight and passion about how they can be of help to their customers. The Micro-Marketer persona enables sellers to build the situational expertise they need to differentiate themselves from other sellers. They do this by managing and nurturing their understanding of buyers, and in so doing, developing better relationships with them. The result is a greater propensity for developing new opportunities as they emerge early in the buying process.

Marketing Automation as a Micro-Marketing Tool   A marketing automation system (MAS) can be an effective nurturing tool for Micro-Marketers, enabling them to foster the development of potential buyer relationships. A MAS allows for the creation of nurturing campaigns that will automatically send relevant content to potential buyers based on trigger events, such as downloading a white paper or signing up for a webinar. These applications score the levels and types of interaction of early-stage buyers with the seller's organization, and encourage higher levels of engagement by providing useful content based on explicitly expressed or implied buyer interests.

Historically, leads were given to sellers to qualify—not a bad idea, if the person who expressed interest was ready to buy. However, this is not always the case. MAS applications such as Marketo, Eloqua, and Pardot can help nurture "not yet sales-ready" leads to the point where it makes sense to transfer them to sellers. Figure 4.4 shows a sample nurturing campaign dashboard screen from a MAS system from Pardot, a Salesforce.com company.

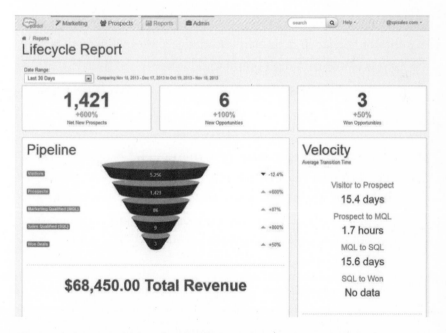

Figure 4.4   Example of a Marketing Automation System

Enabling the Micro-Marketer Persona

Even though the Micro-Marketer persona is very useful for engaging early with Buyer 2.0, we find that many sellers are nevertheless uncomfortable with this persona and developing their own personal brand. Some sellers believe that branding and buyer interest stimulation should be consigned to their organization's marketing department. They fear that by taking on the Micro-Marketer persona, they may be overstepping into job responsibilities that are claimed exclusively by marketing.

Sellers may also lack the technical know-how for logging into and participating in the social web, where Buyer 2.0 is having conversations. They may assume that this is a technical subject that is best left to social media experts in the marketing team.

More commonly, sellers who avoid becoming Micro-Marketers simply don't know what to say that would be of interest to their buyers. Either they have not yet developed sufficient situational fluency or they lack the confidence in their own knowledge and experience to believe that buyers would find their opinions of value.

In order to overcome these obstacles, organizations should consider the following:

- Sales and marketing management must publicly embrace the Micro-Marketer persona for sellers by establishing company policies that provide sellers with the authority to develop their own "brands of one." Managers should allay concerns about the appropriate use of social media by establishing clear guidelines for social media ownership and content.

- Because situational fluency and the confidence to apply it with buyers is the foundation of being a Micro-Marketer, training and educational content on buyers' industries, business issues, and best practices should be made available to sellers—in addition to training on product and service capabilities.

- Next, identifying relevant social media tools and technologies and mapping them to execution of specific Micro-Marketer sales activities can give sellers a logical framework for knowing when to execute these methods and what tools to use to do so.

- Provision of relevant social web tools to sellers, along with any required training on their proper use, will enable sellers to accept and execute the Micro-Marketer persona with more proficiency.

- Finally, charging the marketing team with the development of suitable thought leadership content for use by sellers can help to "prime the pump" of material for use in Micro-Marketing activities, and sustain it as an ongoing practice.

In some regulated industries, such as health care or financial services, the boundaries of what a seller can or cannot say to a buyer are strictly defined. But even under these kinds of restrictions, organizations can help their sellers to be effective Micro-Marketers and develop their own personal brand with their customers. Technologies such as rFactr's SocialPort application can be used to distribute approved content for use in conversations with Buyer 2.0 and still meet regulatory requirements (see Figures 4.5 and 4.6). This puts more responsibility on product and strategic marketing teams to create that content, of course, but it ensures legal compliance while still helping sellers to engage with Buyer 2.0 early in the buying cycles.

While essential in regulated industries, this kind of social media messaging management application can be a boon to any company in any industry. If embraced by content creators in the marketing team, such applications can help improve sellers' confidence levels in their communications with Buyer 2.0. They can also increase the speed at which sellers develop situational fluency—and thus help sellers to establish effective personal brands as Micro-Marketers to Buyer 2.0.

The Micro-Marketer is the first of three personae in *The Collaborative Sale*. It overlaps with and supports the next seller persona required to succeed with Buyer 2.0: the *Visualizer*.

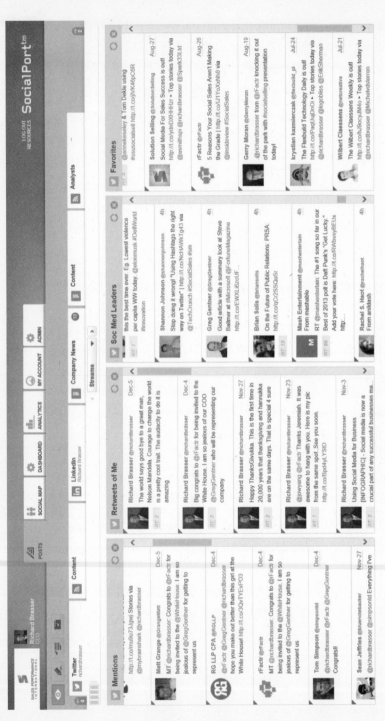

Figure 4.5 Example of a Social Messaging Management System

The content management screen from the rFactr SocialPort application, which allows sellers to monitor social media posts and content relevant to their interests.

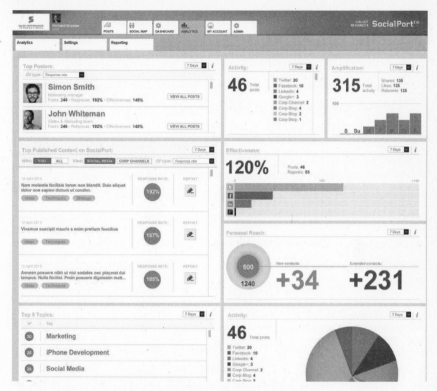

Figure 4.6 Example of Social Media Analytics
The rFactr SocialPort dashboard screen, which displays useful analytics about social media activity.

Corporate Assistance for Micro-Marketers

One of our clients, Emerson Process Management, has combined the roles of chief blogger and head of social media into one full-time position. This role monitors and facilitates the user community called Emerson Exchange 365.[6]

(continued)

---

[6]http://community.emerson.com/process/emerson-exchange/.

Emerson Exchange 365 offers depth and breadth on best practices, technical specifications, and industry-specific forums, where even competitors have been known to "lurk." The platform includes a live tweet stream from both employees and customers, and is especially active during trade shows and user exchanges.

Using Twitter, a prospective buyer who just saw a picture of a newly installed valve might reach out to the person who posted the tweet to ask if it was difficult to install or how it compared to the valve it replaced, for example.

A competitor whose valve was replaced in this Twitter discussion might use this information to research misunderstandings about his company's product, or look up other customers using the same valve in their processes and educate them about proper care and cleaning, so that the customers don't blame the valve company for its poor performance and replace it with an Emerson product, too.

Does David Ivester, Emerson's area vice president for sales in the U.S. Gulf area, care that competitors are watching? No, he laughs: "Let the competitors see why they want to work for Emerson."[7]

When researching this book, we even saw people posting about their career status on Emerson Exchange 365, including an engineering manager whose plant just closed, eliciting a quick reply from Emerson directing him to the company's LinkedIn community.

---

[7]SPI telephone interview with David Ivester, Emerson Process Management, September 19, 2013.

Assisting New Micro-Marketers

Control Southern, an Emerson Process Management business partner, dipped its proverbial toe into the social selling waters in the summer of 2013 when it hired Alex Boss, a recent graduate from the University of Georgia, as a marketing intern—and a marketing department of one.

Emerson Process Management maintains a lively social media presence, and Alex harnessed its tailwinds to help Control Southern's sales force jump into social selling. She began by interviewing Emerson's chief blogger and head of social media to prioritize her tasks and then created a Control Southern company profile on LinkedIn. She immediately started reposting articles there that were originally posted on the Emerson Exchange site to the LinkedIn page. Control Southern offers its customers several training courses, so Alex listed them on the company's page and account managers began sharing them on the platform, an easy way to begin using the service.

During the last company meeting, she brought in a photographer so that everyone would have a professional head shot, and then provided a best practices document for using the site. "Some people still don't know how to use it, but the younger ones are into it," she says. Sellers are starting to reshare articles from Control Southern's page with their networks, and more are using the platform to research what their buyers are talking about online before they make their calls.

When Control Southern picked up a new product line, Alex wrote a press release and distributed it through PR Web. She optimized it for media sharing and carefully monitored

(continued)

headline impressions and the total number of times it was read. She posted the release on Control Southern's LinkedIn page, and some of the account managers said, "This is great; I can promote this at a specific plant."

"I was pleased with the results," Alex says. "Our headline was featured in certain industry segments, and better yet, an account manager got a call based on the release."

Alex spends a considerable amount of time supporting the team in writing quantified business results (QBRs). Control Southern's salespeople are required to document a certain number per year, but until Alex was hired they weren't doing anything with them except store them—and that's a waste.

Following the format of challenge-solution-results, she worked with reps and their customers to write the QBRs and get them approved with customers. She then inserted them into a template using Control Southern's logo and colors. "This content repository will serve the firm and its customers for many years to come," she says.

Her next step will be to publish the QBRs on the company's website, and then share them on LinkedIn and Twitter. Although some corporate policies require anonymity in the QBRs, Alex reports that customers are eager to share how Control Southern provided valuable solutions to their needs. "Our goal is to achieve trusted adviser status," she says, "and a QBR helps us do just that."[8]

[8] SPI telephone interview with Alex Boss, Control Southern, November 4, 2013.

Micro-Marketer Competencies

The Micro-Marketer persona requires sellers to possess or develop a number of key competencies—knowledge, skills, or abilities that enable them to perform the required behaviors for this persona. Managers implementing the Collaborative Sale should look for evidence of these competencies in any potential new hire, and examine what competencies need to be developed in existing sellers on staff.

- *Situational knowledge*—understands the buyer's industry, job roles, areas of responsibility, and common business issues.

- *Capability knowledge*—understands product and service solutions, and how they address customer business issues or capitalize on potential opportunities.

- *Demand creation*—creates and uses business development messaging for generating demand, providing thought leadership, and stimulating buyer interest.

- *Problem needs identification*—identifies buyers' business drivers for change within a targeted market, organization, prospect, or opportunity.

- *Communication skills*—has ability to express points of view clearly, both orally and in written form.

- *Networking and relationship-building skills*—is able to build productive social bonds with customers and buyers; builds, maintains, and leverages mutually beneficial business relationships.

(continued)

- *Social media utilization*—uses social media tools to expand seller's knowledge and to interact with and influence buyers.

- *Technical skills*—is able to use appropriate technology to participate in social web and online customer conversations, as well as any supporting Micro-Marketer technologies, such as a marketing automation system.

- *Planning and organizational skills*—can use structured processes and methods to identify a logical sequence of events and activities required to achieve an intended goal or result.

The Story (Continued)

The Delta Sky Club lounge felt stale to Jon. He wanted to pace the floor and walk off some of his energy that had accumulated during the past hour.

Nancy said, "Tell me what you're doing to market yourself as a thought leader in this space, Jon."

Time stood still.

Eventually Jon said, "Nancy, I've been 100 percent focused on getting appointments and riding on airplanes. I don't have time to speak at conferences."

"What are you doing on LinkedIn?"

"I have a profile and I use it for research. Why?"

"You don't have to speak at conferences to market yourself as a thought leader. You can do it right there on LinkedIn. I'll send you a link to a great webinar on how to get started."

A week later, after watching the Micro-Marketer webinar, Jon decided that every Sunday night, when his wife turned to *Masterpiece*

Theater, he would turn to LinkedIn for an hour or two of personal brand building. He had no particular love for the period drama series that was currently running, but his wife enjoyed his company even if he wasn't following the plot with her.

Reading the insurance broker's LinkedIn updates, he shouldn't have been surprised to see that the broker shared a familiar white paper in his stream. Nancy had sent him the link to the same report when they met in the airport the previous week.

Jon's first thought was: Damn—I should have been the one who introduced him to that white paper.

He shook off the self-recriminations and went back to research ideas for how to build his pipeline and personal brand. He noticed that most of his insurance prospects belonged to a group that was facilitated by a PhD statistician with a keen interest in weather patterns, so he spent an hour scrolling through the threads and downloading a couple of white papers along the way. He scheduled time with himself to read the materials and decide which prospects would appreciate the information.

The threads also yielded five prospects Jon had never spoken to. He thought, I'll see how to get in their line of vision tomorrow.

Next, he looked at the groups that his two strongest competitors belonged to and monitored how they were conducting themselves. One used a lot of sports metaphors to kick off discussions, and Jon grudgingly admired how smoothly the competitor interjected that he used his software to help him pick his fantasy league players, even though that wasn't the software's intended use. That's working for him, Jon thought, but I'm not going down that road.

Another competitor frequently shared decks from conferences he attended. Very few of them were from the competitor's personal presentations; he shared decks from other panelists as well. Jon had recently watched a webinar that stressed the importance of curating content, and not merely pushing materials from ExyRisk. Jon noticed that his competitor didn't just share the decks generally; instead, to save potential readers the aggravation of scrolling through the entire deck, he advised group members which specific slides related to an active discussion.

I can do that, Jon thought, as he rummaged through his backpack for a thumb drive of decks from the conference he'd attended a week ago. Not only can I do this on LinkedIn, but I can also e-mail one of these to a couple of prospects who didn't go to the conference.

5 The Visualizer Persona

Through all of human history, people have longed to know their future. In ancient Greece, rulers came to Delphi on the slopes of Mount Parnassus to speak to the Oracle, in hopes that she would dispense profound visions of their coming fates. So highly valued were these visions that people made long and arduous journeys just for the opportunity to hear them.

The power of vision still stirs people to action. Buyers with a clear picture of how they can solve a problem or take advantage of a new opportunity are motivated to purchase the capabilities needed to realize their visions. Conversely, if they cannot envision a better future state, then they certainly will not take action.

The difference depends on a seller's own vision, and the ability to help buyers see that compelling vision of their future—one that enables buyers to see how they can use new capabilities to realize tangible value. Sellers who have this ability are *Visualizers*.

What Is a Visualizer?

The Visualizer persona enables a seller to see what could be, help buyers see this vision for themselves, and make that vision so compelling that buyers are willing to take action.

To be a proficient Visualizer, sellers must know how to engage in useful conversations with buyers, whether those conversations are online, in person, or over the telephone. This is how buyers form opinions and perceptions about sellers, their personal brand, their company, and the value they bring to a buyer's situation. Sellers who collaborate to create compelling visions of future states distinguish themselves from other sellers—not only by *what* they sell, but also by *how* they sell.

Visualizers Are Fountains of Useful Ideas

Buyer 2.0 has little patience with sellers who do not bring insightful perspectives about how to solve problems and create value. Starting with the very first online interaction, telephone discussion, or face-to-face meeting, sellers who cannot bring new points of view are eliminated quickly from further consideration. Sellers who can't offer new or innovative ways to solve customer problems are perceived only as salespeople or vendors of products, not as useful and trusted advisers. The question is whether this type of seller will have a job in the future.[1] Currently, we see the number of sellers declining in developed markets. Anyone who does not add value in the supply chain of business is being eliminated.[2]

Visualizers are creative freethinkers, and they often consider unconventional approaches to problems and opportunities.

---

[1]"Fifteen Million Salespeople to Be Displaced by 2020, Predicts Sales 2.0 Conference Host," *Reuters U.S. News*, Thomson Reuters News Service, March 15, 2011. Accessed December 1, 2013, at www.reuters.com/article/2011/03/15/idUS233420 15-Mar-2011. *Selling Power* magazine publisher Gerhard Gschwandtner predicts that the number of sellers in the United States will decline from 18 million to fewer than 3 million by 2020.

[2]James Ledbetter, Death of a Salesman. Of Lots of Them, Actually *Slate* Magazine, "Moneybox," September 21, 2010. Accessed December 1, 2013, at www.slate.com/articles/business/moneybox/2010/09/death_of_a_salesman_of_lots_of_them_actually.html.

They serve buyers by helping them envision what *could* be, and they don't limit the components of their potential vision to capabilities from their own company. They are comfortable in establishing or engaging partnerships and alliances to get the job done for their customers, if required.

The cornerstone competency for the Visualizer persona is *situational fluency*, which we defined in Chapter 3 as critical to mastering all three personae in *The Collaborative Sale*. Situational fluency is the combination of situational knowledge, capability knowledge, people skills, selling skills, and a willing attitude to engage collaboratively. Without situational fluency, sellers won't have sufficient knowledge about the buyer to develop their own visions of what could be, and they will lack the skills to convey a vision in a compelling way to the buyer.

Drawing from their situational fluency, Visualizers develop informed opinions, and they are not afraid of sharing their viewpoints with buyers. Visualizers fearlessly imagine creative and innovative hypotheses about how they can help buyers to solve problems or capitalize on potential opportunities, and then test and refine the potential value of those ideas in conversations with buyers.

Visualizers Create Compelling Visions of the Future

Visualizers also help buyers see ideas in a compelling way—not only so buyers can understand that potential future state, but also so that they are highly motivated to achieve it. Visualizers have a unique ability to see possible futures. They can conduct what-if analyses on the fly—and can couch or phrase something in such a way that it captures the imagination and interest of buyers.

Salespeople who are Visualizers love their craft, are passionate about learning and growing, and are focused on helping customers solve real problems.

For example, one of our clients is a provider of gaseous element products to its customers. The company sells oxygen, hydrogen, helium, and other so-called pure gases for use in industrial and health care applications. The firm asked us to look at the sales team to see what kind of improvements could be made in their performance. As part of this project, we had the opportunity to observe one of their top-performing sales representatives, who specialized in selling to hospitals. We'll call him Steven here.

Steven sold almost twice as much as every other seller in the company, and he had done so for several years. We found him in his office, doing some online research on several hospitals located in an area he intended to call on. "Come on," he said. "It's time to hit the road."

We assumed he had made some appointments with prospects, but we soon learned that wasn't the case. "No, this is in-the-field research," he said. "The meetings with the customer will come later."

We arrived at the hospital. Steven asked at the front desk for directions to the intensive care unit. After a quick introduction to one of the nurses there, he asked a few questions, such as the number of beds in the unit and the kinds of cases they managed. It took only a few minutes.

"Okay, time to go around back," he said. We then went outside, and walked around to the rear of the building, where a large cylindrical tank was stationed. "This is their bulk oxygen storage, and it's useful that I'm able to get this close," he said with a wink. He snapped a few pictures of the tank with the camera on his smart phone.

"Back to the car now," he announced, heading to the parking lot. He launched Google Maps on his phone and said, "We are here." He pinched the screen around that point, studying it intently. "That's a five-mile radius—that should be enough." He continued zooming, pinching, and studying his screen for a few minutes, quietly. "Yeah, this is good," he said. "There's a strong case here."

We weren't sure what he was talking about, but he seemed pleased. "Back to the office now," he said. "We have work to do."

Once there, Steven started his computer and began to enter figures into a spreadsheet. "It's time to let you in on a little secret," he confessed. "I don't sell gases to hospitals."

That made us curious. What *did* he sell, then?

"Almost all of the other reps in this company sell a commodity product, primarily to the purchasing manager. They approach the sale by offering a lower price, determined by the distance between the customer and our nearest manufacturing plant," he explained. "Instead, I sell a solution to a critical business problem—risk mitigation in a hospital. Risk mitigation is worth much more, and buyers of risk reduction aren't in the purchasing department. I sell it to executives who own that problem. That's the difference between me and most of the other reps here."

He showed us the results of his spreadsheet. He had calculated the amount of oxygen currently used by the hospital, based on his questions and observations. "Now, on the map there are five light industrial and two heavy manufacturing factories nearby. One of them is a chemical plant, in fact. There are about 5,000 employees there. If there was a serious accident at any one of those locations—an explosion or a dangerous chemical leak, for example—then this hospital could see a lot of hurt people."

He tapped a number on his computer screen with the cap of his ballpoint pen. "They could need as much oxygen as this, given that number of cases and their total number of beds." Looking away from the screen and at us, he shook his head. "They don't have nearly that much now."

Steven went on with his analysis, estimating the number of potential injuries and deaths that the oxygen shortage might create, and the potential risk of financial losses from resulting lawsuits. The number was tens of millions of dollars.

"And what's more," he continued, "they have some significant safety issues, too." Showing us the pictures he snapped, he pointed out a few problems, including the fact that security was so lax. "This is a crisis just waiting to happen, and I'll bet they don't even know it yet."

Steven sent his analysis of the risks and safety issues to the hospital's chief administration officer (CAO), and soon got an appointment. The CAO was alarmed by the dreary picture of a possible future full of litigation and financial costs.

We want to emphasize that Steven was not using a scare tactic; he was genuine in his approach and he identified a real problem. He suggested a vision of how the hospital could avoid such a fate with an adequate and reliable supply from a firm that could provide expertise in delivering the right amounts while also doing so safely—his firm. Within a couple of weeks, he won a very sizable service contract, and a very satisfied customer.

Let's be clear about why Steven was successful. It wasn't because he sold "better" gas in "better" tanks. His products are a commodity sale in that regard. He won because he was willing to do research, identify a problem the buyers didn't know existed, and enable them to see their world free from the risk of a potentially difficult situation. This Visualizer made a difference to his customers in ways they had not yet considered before he entered their lives.

The Visualizer persona requires a combination of clarity, creativity, confidence, courage, and communication skills. Like Steven, those who develop these abilities can become adept at helping Buyer 2.0 envision a better future state—one enabled by the seller's unique or highly differentiated capabilities, which include *how the seller interacts with the buyer*. A Visualizer's conversation can be enough of a differentiator to win Buyer 2.0's business.

Buyer States and Strength of Vision

The previous example of the gas products seller illustrates how a Visualizer can initiate a new opportunity with a buyer. However, Buyer 2.0 typically engages sellers after they have begun to form their own vision. The Visualizer persona helps sellers to engage effectively with late stage buyers as well, by further enhancing or re-engineering their existing visions.

In one of our previous books, *The New Solution Selling*, we examined behavior from two different perspectives: buyers who are not actively looking for a solution and those who are.

The first type of buyer behavior we labeled "not looking." The typical reasons for buyers being in this state are because of ignorance or rationalization. In other words, they are not yet aware of problems or opportunities that could be solved or taken advantage of, or they may be aware but lack a clear vision of what they can or should do about it.

The second type of buyer behavior we labeled "looking." The typical reason for buyers being in this state is because they are aware of the problem or opportunity facing them; they have clear vision of what actions to take. They are actively seeking solutions to their problems or ways that they can capitalize on an emerging opportunity.

The reason for making this distinction was to help sellers understand these buyer patterns and to assist them with strategies and techniques for dealing with the different buyer behaviors.

While it is still possible to find buyers who are "not looking" and jointly develop a vision of what could be, it is becoming increasingly uncommon because Buyer 2.0 typically develops their own vision first, before engaging any sellers.

We previously thought that if a seller found a buyer who was already "looking" and the seller didn't help create the buyer's vision, the seller should assume that a competitor did. The logic was sound because it allowed the seller to choose a winning strategy; that is, the seller focused on changing the buyer's vision by introducing new criteria into the decision. Otherwise, the sellers had to compete against a vision they didn't create, which gave them little chance of winning.

Before the proliferation of the Internet, buyers developed visions of potential solutions primarily from information provided by sellers. Since most organizations cannot make a purchase without looking at multiple options, buyers contacted additional sellers so that they could complete all the required columns on an evaluation matrix. In other words, most sellers brought into an active evaluation were being used as "column fodder" and had a much lower chance of winning compared to the seller organization that had helped the buyer to first develop the vision.

However, Buyer 2.0 is no longer dependent upon sellers for information about potential solutions. Now buyers can find much of what they need on their own. As a result, buyers are less influenced by sellers and are more likely to develop their own vision of a potential solution before contacting any seller. Sellers should not assume that a buyer's vision is purely a result of competitor influence.

Further, the strength of the buyer's vision can vary significantly, depending on when a seller first engages with Buyer 2.0. The state of a buyer vision may range from barely existent to completely defined. The Visualizer persona begins with understanding the strength of a buyer vision—that is, how malleable it is, and how open the buyer is to having that vision shaped and refined further.

Therefore, engaging effectively with Buyer 2.0 now requires a more nuanced understanding of the buyer's state when first encountered by a seller, as illustrated in Figure 5.1.

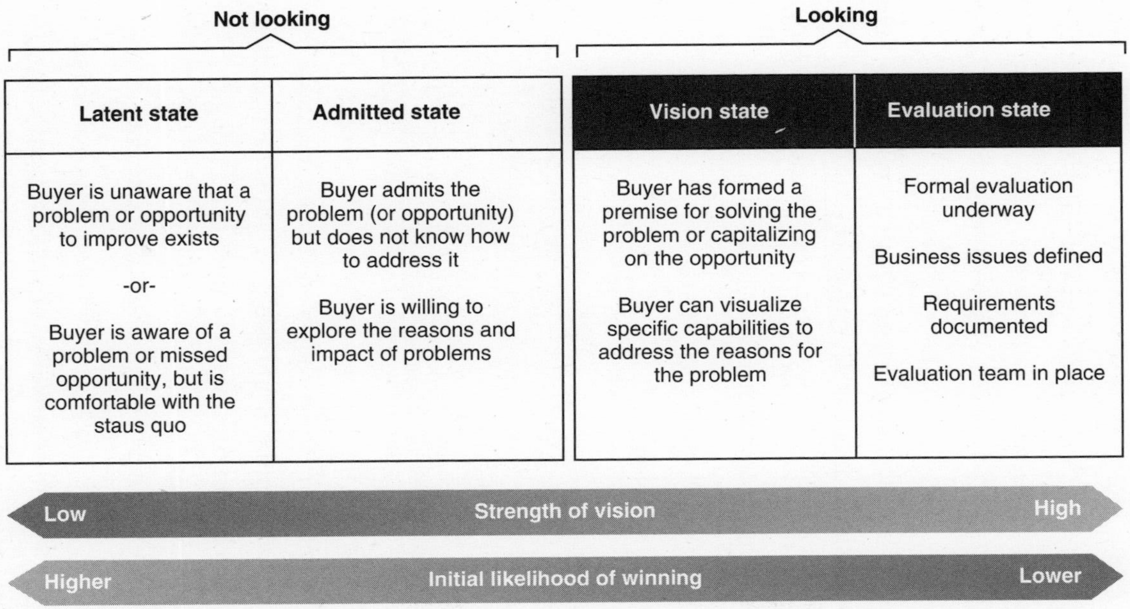

Not looking		Looking	
Latent state	**Admitted state**	**Vision state**	**Evaluation state**
Buyer is unaware that a problem or opportunity to improve exists -or- Buyer is aware of a problem or missed opportunity, but is comfortable with the staus quo	Buyer admits the problem (or opportunity) but does not know how to address it Buyer is willing to explore the reasons and impact of problems	Buyer has formed a premise for solving the problem or capitalizing on the opportunity Buyer can visualize specific capabilities to address the reasons for the problem	Formal evaluation underway Business issues defined Requirements documented Evaluation team in place

Strength of vision: Low → High

Initial likelihood of winning: Higher → Lower

Figure 5.1 Buyer States

Buyer 2.0 may be found in one of four states, corresponding with the strength of vision, from low to high:

- *"Not looking."* The buyer is not actively seeking a solution to a problem or a way to capitalize on a potential opportunity.

  ◆ *Latent state.* The buyer is unaware that a problem or an opportunity exists, or is aware but is willing to live with the status quo.

  ◆ *Admitted state.* The buyer admits that a problem or an opportunity exists, but does not yet know how to address it.

- *"Looking."* The buyer is actively exploring ways to solve a problem or take advantage of an emerging opportunity.

  ◆ *Vision state.* The buyer has begun to form ideas for addressing a problem or an opportunity, but has not yet identified all the capabilities required.

  ◆ *Evaluation state.* The buyer has a fully formed vision and has begun a formal review of potential alternatives.

Even if buyers in a "not looking" state are aware of a problem or potential opportunity, they may be so overwhelmed with data about potential options that they do not know whether or how they might improve their situation. Today, buyers who remain stuck in an admitted state are usually confused and paralyzed into inaction, because they do not fully understand the implications of continuing to maintain the status quo. In other words, they do not yet have a clear vision in their minds, and the Visualizer can help them to create one.

For buyers who already have developed an initial vision, the Visualizer should think of it like an elastic band. An elastic band has little value on its own; however, once it is stretched, it has many applications: to hold things together, to shoot across the room, or to secure an item in place. The self-discovered vision of a buyer is analogous to an as-yet-unstretched elastic band. The Visualizer's job is to stretch the vision of buyers—to let them see new or additional possibilities of what could be.

At no point should a Visualizer criticize buyers for their vision. The Visualizer does not openly challenge a vision or create conflict, but instead seeks to understand the buyer's current vision and then collaborate with the buyer to share and explore useful ideas for improvement. Only then can great things be achieved.

Visualizer Conversations

The kinds of conversations that a Visualizer has with Buyer 2.0 to develop a more complete vision of an optimized solution will vary according to the state of the buyer. For example, when buyers are in a "not looking" state, either latent or admitted, they need help in creating a clear vision of a solution. This is exactly what the gas products seller did in our previous example. He helped the buyer recognize a problem (i.e., risk exposure) and establish a vision of how the hospital could safely and affordably avoid those potential costs.

Buyer 2.0, however, generally engages sellers after they have developed an initial vision. But simply accepting a buyer's vision at face value provides no value to Buyer 2.0. If a buyer is still formulating ideas for a possible solution, but the strength of that vision is not yet fully articulated, the seller can capture and confirm that vision, and then enhance the vision and improve upon it. If a buyer's vision is well established and documented, the seller can acknowledge that vision, and then attempt to reengineer it in part or in total, in order to explore better or incrementally improved ways of addressing the problem or potential opportunity. Remember the elastic band—sellers who simply react to Buyer 2.0 are not stretching their thinking. They make no real difference.

The Visualizer persona enables sellers to:

- See for themselves the possibilities of what could be.
- Enable buyers to see this vision.
- Make that vision compelling so buyers are willing to take action.

Visualizers accomplish this in their conversations with Buyer 2.0. Conversations are the principal form of communication between buyers and sellers. And, since buying behavior has changed, it makes sense that the nature of sales conversations must also change. Equipping sellers with a new conversation model and supporting tools becomes a priority for effectively executing collaborative conversations.

When engaging in collaborative conversations, sellers must keep an open mind, ask insightful questions, and bring an informed point of view to the table. The main objectives of the conversation are to understand their current situation (good or bad) and the reasons for the situation, and to explore the capabilities that will produce a better future state. Every conversation should start with the perspectives of the buyer, then introduce the perspectives of the seller, and then jointly collaborate to develop a mutually enhanced and agreed-upon perspective. The structure of a collaborative conversation is simple, and can be illustrated as shown in Figure 5.2.

There are multiple paths that can be taken through the collaborative sales conversation structure, depending on the state of the buyer and the strength of the buyer's initial vision. The three types of collaborative sales conversations, with their respective applicabilities to different buyer states (illustrated in Figure 5.3), are:

1. *Vision creation*—for establishing an initial vision jointly with the buyer.
2. *Vision enhancement*—for capturing and expanding upon an emerging vision of the buyer.

3. *Vision reengineering*—for exploring alternative options for an improved buyer vision.

A *vision creation* conversation is most useful when speaking with buyers in a latent or admitted state. It begins after identifying a potential problem, critical business issue, or opportunity, and gaining agreement with the buyer to explore the implications of the current

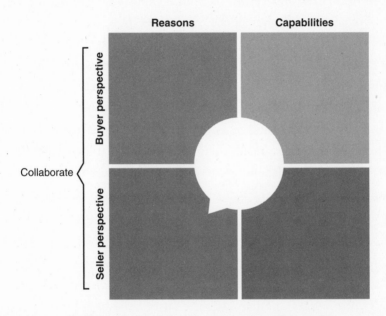

Figure 5.2 Collaborative Sales Conversation Structure

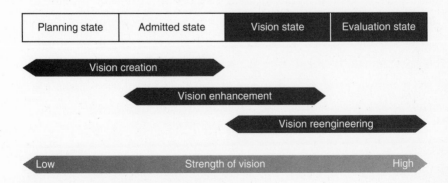

Figure 5.3 Visualizer Conversations

situation. At that point, sellers can prompt buyers to share their perspective on the underlying reasons for the current situation. The sellers can then demonstrate their situational fluency by exploring any additional factors that may be contributing to the current state. The seller and buyer can then capture and agree upon a mutual understanding of the reasons for the current situation.

After the relevant reasons have been captured, buyers can then share their perspective about the capabilities they envision are needed to improve upon the current state. The seller can then share a perspective on those capabilities, or suggest new or different capabilities that might help, by asking, "When doing X, if you could do Y, would that be of help in addressing the problem or reaching your goal?" Once again, both the buyer and seller can then collaborate to arrive at a mutually agreed-upon vision that will address the underlying reasons for the problem, critical business issue, or potential opportunity.

A *vision enhancement* conversation is most useful with helping a buyer with a vision that is not yet fully formed, typically when the buyer is in an admitted or early vision state. Instead of starting with a potential problem, critical business issue, or opportunity, this conversation begins with first capturing an understanding of the current buyer vision, and the capabilities the buyer believes are required. The seller can then ask the buyer to share the buyer's perspective about the underlying reasons for the vision, and can then provide the seller's own perspective by exploring any additional factors that may be contributing to the current situation. After coming to a mutual agreement on the reasons for the current situation with the buyer, the seller can then suggest enhancements and expanded capabilities for the buyer's initial vision. The buyer and seller can then come to an agreement on an enhanced vision.

A *vision reengineering* conversation is similar to vision enhancement, except it explores options for improving upon a strong buyer vision. This is useful for conversing with buyers in vision or active evaluation states. As in vision enhancement, the conversation begins with capturing an understanding of the current buyer vision and the capabilities the buyer believes are required. The intent of the seller, however, is somewhat different. The seller may then suggest alternative visions, not just additional or enhanced capabilities, that solve the buyer's problem in a different but better way, or that will help the buyer to capitalize better on an emerging opportunity. In short, in vision reengineering, the seller is bringing a fresh perspective that is more comprehensive than simply adding to or improving on the buyer's initial vision. In this case, the seller is exploring alternative approaches that may change the vision significantly, but also produce better results.

Vision reengineering is the most difficult of the three collaborative sales conversations because it must be done tactfully, and from a very informed point of view based on strong situational fluency of the seller. Seller credibility is critical. Buyers should never feel that the seller is trying to force an alternative that is not in their best interests. Rather, the seller must be able to show the connection between the underlying reasons for the problem or potential opportunity and the improved capabilities of the suggested alternative approach. If the buyer and seller can agree on a reengineered vision, then the likelihood of the seller winning that business is very significantly improved.

Embracing the Visualizer Persona

As we said at the beginning of this chapter, the power of vision stirs people to action. The Visualizer persona enables sellers to apply their situational fluency to:

- See the possibilities of what could be for themselves.
- Enable buyers to see this vision.
- Make that vision compelling so buyers are willing to take action.

However, even if the Visualizer develops a powerful vision of a solution in collaboration with a buyer, it is still possible that the buyer may not make a purchase decision. That is because Buyer 2.0 is also highly sensitive to risk, which may stall or completely paralyze the buying decision. As a result, there is one more essential persona required for collaborative sellers: the *Value Driver*, which we explore in the next chapter.

Visualizer Competencies

The Visualizer persona requires sellers to possess or develop a number of key competencies—knowledge, skills, or abilities that enable them to perform the required behaviors for this persona. Managers implementing the Collaborative Sale should look for evidence of these competencies in any potential new hire, and examine what competencies need to be developed in existing sellers on staff.

- *Situational knowledge*—understands the buyer's industry, job roles, areas of responsibility, and common business issues.
- *Capability knowledge*—understands product and service solutions, and how they address customer business issues or capitalize on potential opportunities.
- *Communication skills*—has ability to express points of view clearly, both orally and in written form.
- *Sales conversation skills*—collaboratively diagnoses buyer problems or potential opportunities; creates, expands, or reengineers visions of solutions; develops mutual agreement with buyers on capabilities needed.

- *Opportunity qualification*—applies guiding standards to assess the correct buyer state, strength of buyer vision, and quality of a sales opportunity, and then make engagement and prioritization decisions.

- *Competitive skills*—evaluates competitive positions and executes appropriate strategies and tactics to win.

- *Relationship-building skills*—is able to build productive social bonds with customers and buyers; builds, maintains, and leverages mutually beneficial business relationships.

- *Customer focus*—keeps the customer foremost in mind; advocates for the customer's best interests.

The Story (Continued)

Jon always opened his e-mail first thing in the morning, even before getting out of bed. Nothing important had come through in the past six hours except Nancy's meeting request for the following week, when she would be in town for a board meeting. Thinking back to their first meeting at the airport, he could see how her advice to delay asking for demos had worked for him. She had pulled a file out of her black monogrammed messenger bag, and placed a thick presentation between them, thumbing to the fifth page.

"Here's what another of our portfolio companies is doing with collaboration. Yesterday, Bowsi's lead business development guy had a first meeting with A-Bank. Of course, Bowsi is selling something different from ExyRisk, but let's set that aside. It's the approach of the Bowsi seller that I admire."

Nancy had tapped a column of calculations with her forefinger. "He relied on the world's universal language, numbers. He did his homework and extrapolated from another engagement while estimating the size of the bank's mortgage portfolio based on a Hoover's report," she had explained.

"Then he calculated the ROI on Bowsi's Tier One product using one-, three-, and four-year horizons," she had said, tapping the respective columns.

Nancy had met Jon's eyes. "Remember, he did all that just to get the first appointment. When he got into the meeting, the bankers quizzed him on his methodology and poked at his case study. When they were satisfied, they told them that although the numbers he extrapolated weren't precise, the formulas and his approach were intriguing, so they asked for a demo."

Jon had studied the page and nodded. "I see that. Well done."

"Now I want to show you a tool that Bowsi is using to collaborate with prospects; it's called VisualizeROI." She had opened her laptop and let it warm up. "Instead of building a spreadsheet model on your computer, I want you to build it in this tool. It has all the muscle you need but it will help you collaborate with your prospects in some intriguing ways."

She had fired up the application and they had watched the demo together. The wheels had turned in Jon's head as he watched.

At the end, he had said, "I'll go back and say I've calculated that a partnership with us has a bigger impact than he thinks. Let's say I've come up with a $20 million improvement over four years, if my assumptions are valid. I can build a model to that number, for sure."

"Great start, but hold on just a second," Nancy had said, reaching for her phone and tapping the screen. "I just figured there are 1,460 days in four years. You could say, 'Based on what I'm seeing, every day we don't take action is $20 million divided by 1,460, which is nearly $14,000 of lost revenue each day.'"

"Yeah, I can take this and run with it," Jon had said. He had paused as a doubt arose: "What if it's not $20 million, but less? Haven't I shot myself in the foot with a big number?"

"As long as you collaborate on your assumptions, like the Bowsi rep did, you're fine. He will probably say, 'That's a bit aggressive—let's scale it back to some other number,' but now he owns that other number. The next step would be to prove you can deliver on that, and then you go to a demo."

Jon had shifted in his chair and looked at the ceiling, "Of course another approach would be to say, 'I'd like to talk to you about validating my assumptions. It might be more compelling than it looks.'"

"Now you're talking," Nancy had said, smiling. "There's this concept I've heard sales consultants use called situational fluency, a blend of people skills, selling skills, capability knowledge, situational knowledge, and a willingness to collaborate. Do some homework and see if this firm would respond better to an opening volley of 'I can help you make $20 million over the next four years' compared to 'I'd like to validate some assumptions I've made that might mean that a partnership with us is worth $20 million to you over the next four years.'"

6 The Value Driver Persona

By perfecting the innovative idea of containerization in global transport, Maersk Line became the leading container shipping company in the world. By 2011, the company had grown to more than $25 billion in revenues, with 325 offices in 125 countries, and 22,000 employees serving over 100,000 customers worldwide, using a fleet of ships carrying over 1.6 million container units.

But Maersk Line was at a crossroads, facing some unsettling realities. New competitors were emerging. Customers increasingly perceived container shipping space as a commodity, and rate wars were eroding profits. The shipping giant knew its proud legacy was no guarantee of future success and continued industry leadership. Something had to change.

So, in 2011 Maersk leadership produced a stunning proposal entitled *The New Normal: A Manifesto for Changing the Way We Think about Shipping*.[1] It was bold and innovative, but more important, it confronted the brutal facts. The manifesto conceded that the industry's 50-year-old protocol was letting customers down. Shipping

---

[1] A copy of this document, *The New Normal: A Manifesto for Changing the Way We Think about Shipping*, can be downloaded from: http://preview .thenewsmarket.com/Previews/MAER/DocumentAssets/207207_v2.pdf.

had settled into a pattern of "good enough" results where containers arrived late as often as they were on time. Simply selling container space at ever lower rates was a race to bottom—a one-way ticket to profitless commoditization.

Maersk leadership boldly stated that "shipping had to be turned on its head." Why couldn't Maersk provide increased value by making *reliability* and *excellent customer service* the new normal in the shipping industry? The company introduced Daily Maersk, an offering developed in direct response to increasing concerns about freight reliability. "Customers had to take out huge buffer stocks to compensate for all of the times a ship didn't arrive on time, so they were losing money by the hour," explains Jesper Thomsen, Global Head of Commercial, Maersk Line.

Daily Maersk introduced the practice of having ships that leave the same port at the same time every day so that at least 95 percent of shipments arrive as scheduled. Considering that the industry standard is 50 percent on-time delivery, Daily Maersk represents a radical shift in mind-set and offers massive cost-saving potential for customers.

But offering compelling new forms of value would matter only if the company's 2,000 salespeople could articulate the value of why twenty-first-century customers should choose Maersk. They asked Sales Performance International (SPI) to help enable their sales team to identify customer business challenges and then quantify and articulate the value of overcoming these issues.

"Now we help customers to consider issues they hadn't thought about before—new ways to improve their business," asserts Eric Williams, Global Head of Sales, Maersk Line. "We move the conversation beyond the standard 'What is your price from Hong Kong to Rotterdam?'" Maersk Line also developed interactive value calculation tools for the sales team, enabling them to provide quantitative estimates of business impact for each customer.

Thomsen estimates that the changes in sales behavior have earned many millions in incremental profits from the new value-driven container sales, but that isn't the only positive result. "What's most important is that we have fundamentally changed the conversation with the customer and helped to decommoditize transportation."

Focusing on Value

Maersk Line is an excellent example of how changing sales behavior from emphasizing *product and price* to emphasizing *solution and value* can make a significant difference to results—for both the seller and the buyer. In less than a year, Maersk Line realized more than $111 million in increased revenue, representing a 350 percent return on investment in the value-driven sales behavior initiative.[2]

Since Buyer 2.0 is highly risk averse, the new buyers will choose to do nothing or stay with the status quo if they don't see specific and compelling value in a seller's proposed solution to their problems or opportunities. What Maersk Line accomplished was to help the sales team mitigate Buyer 2.0's perception of risk by equipping sellers with the methods and tools required to assume the third persona in the collaborative sale—the Value Driver.

What Is the Value Driver Persona?

The Value Driver persona enables a seller to:

- Understand and position value throughout the buying process. That is, they lead with, sell with, and close with value.

- Collaborate with buyers so that the discovery and confirmation of value are jointly determined.

---

[2]Alexandra Levit, "How to Sell Value Instead of Commodities," *Forbes Online*, August 8, 2013. Accessed December 1, 2013, at www.forbes.com/sites/theyec/2013/08/08/how-to-sell-value-instead-of-commodities/.

- Use value to build a compelling business reason to act.
- Use a Collaboration Plan to influence the buying cycle and mitigate risk.

Sellers who take up the Value Driver persona and communicate specific, quantitative value early and throughout engagement with a buyer are more likely to win business. The Value Driver collaborates with individual buyers and buying committees to eliminate fears from a purchase decision.

As buyers progress into an active state of evaluation, they become more concerned with potential risks associated with their possible choices of action. Risk comes in several forms:

- *Operational risk.* Quite simply, will it work? Will the solution provide the capabilities required to reach or exceed business goals?
- *Transitional risk.* How do the buyers get from where they are today to where they are using the solution successfully? What factors need to be considered in implementing the solution? What could go wrong during the transition?
- *Financial risk.* What is the quantitative value of the solution to the organization? How does this compare to alternative uses of funds and resources? Is it a good investment?

The Value Driver recognizes that Buyer 2.0 is concerned with all types of risk, and they take proactive steps to mitigate the risks, making it easier for buyers to progress to a purchase decision. Even if a compelling financial case can be made for an envisioned solution, the qualitative aspects of a purchase cannot be ignored. Operational concerns and transitional issues can block the decision to buy as effectively as the lack of a compelling quantitative case for value.

For example, one of our clients is a provider of typographic technology—electronic typefaces and fonts for use in software applications and consumer electronics display screens. One of its sellers was working with a consumer electronics manufacturer to provide typefaces for an electronic control panel on a new line of household appliances.

The appliance maker agreed that the solution provider's technology would make the line easier to use, and therefore improve sales. The customer's product management team agreed with the seller's estimates of financial value. Since the new technology had been proven in similar applications, there were no operational concerns. In fact, the customer's marketing team believed that the new display technology would make the line highly appealing to consumers, and therefore make it a big seller.

So, the customer agreed the investment was worthwhile, and that the product would fulfill all of its requirements. And yet, the customer was unable to make a decision. The paralyzing issue was that the technology required some new skills in product design. It used a different approach from an older system, one that the customer's engineering team already knew and liked. The engineers were resisting the change, saying that the time needed to learn the new technology would delay the line's market launch.

Only when our client's seller discovered this transition issue was he able to address it. He proposed providing a training expert and some technical consulting to assist with the product design work for the new line. Once concerns about the transitional risk were addressed, the customer signed the contract eagerly.

Finding Compelling Reasons to Act

Buyers do not act without compelling reasons to do so. The Value Driver's mission is to find those reasons. If a reason is bound to a hard deadline—a specific time that a new capability will be required—then the buyer will be compelled to act before that deadline in order to avoid adverse results. For example, another of our clients provides customized information systems for financial investment management and stock brokerage firms. If one of its customers wants to grow revenues by opening a new office, then missing the planned opening date could mean a loss of revenue, budget overruns, and idle workers. For that customer, having the office open on the planned date becomes a compelling reason to act.

Even if there is no obvious time-bound reason to act, the Value Driver can create a compelling case for avoiding delay in a buying decision. If the quantitative value of a potential solution is known, then every day that goes by without those capabilities in place means a loss of those benefits to the buyer. A simple example: if the value gained is estimated to be $1 million annually, then every day of delay costs $5,000, based on 200 workdays per year. The Value Driver persona can help buyers overcome any hesitancy to act by showing them the cost of not taking action and of settling for the status quo.

Eliminating Losses to No Decision

If a seller fails to convey value or mitigate risk, then buyers will hesitate to make a purchase decision, resulting in a loss due to inaction. CSO Insights found in a 2012 survey[3] of sales organizations that nearly one-quarter (24 percent) of all forecasted opportunities ended up as losses due to inaction; in other words, the buyer chose to do nothing at all. For most organizations today, losses to no decision number higher than losses to any direct competitor. The Value Driver persona, if executed well, helps to eliminate losses due to no decision.

Collaborating on Solution Value

It is entirely possible for a seller to win a solution evaluation by Buyer 2.0, but not win business. Even if sellers show how their

---

[3] *Sales Performance Optimization Report*, CSO Insights, 2012. Also at www .csoinsights.com.

capabilities can solve buyers' business problems, and also show how buyers can successfully implement their solutions, Buyer 2.0 is still unlikely to buy without an understanding of the quantitative value and potential return on investment for that solution. The collaborative seller recognizes this need, and works with buyers to develop mutually agreed-upon estimates of value.

To develop a credible estimate of value that buyers can believe in, sellers must first define the scope and impact of a problem or potential missed opportunity. They must determine the adverse effects of their current problem or potential missed opportunity.

- What revenues are being missed, lost, or reduced?
- What costs are being increased or added?
- What risks are being assumed that could otherwise be reduced or avoided?

A Value Driver diagnoses the scope of buyer problems or opportunities by utilizing the conversation model described in the previous chapter. By determining how much, how often, and how many times a buyer experiences the negative implications of a problem or potential missed opportunity, a Value Driver can then develop an estimate of value—a quantitative assessment of the impact of a potential solution.

In working with sellers around the world, we've learned that many of them do not subscribe to or engage in the Value Driver persona. We believe it's because they lack the situational and capability knowledge needed to engage in this activity. Additionally, many of them are not given the tools to do the job. And, if they don't engage in the value analysis process, they certainly can't give buyers a compelling reason to act based on value. CSO Insights' 2012 survey showed that only 16 percent of sales executives believe their teams convey the value of their solutions well.[4]

---

[4]Ibid.

Fortunately, both the sophistication and the ease of use of value estimation tools have improved greatly. Even more important, these emergent value calculation tools are designed to be used collaboratively with buyers, to encourage and enable mutual agreement on estimates of value.

For example, Maersk Line, cited at the beginning of this chapter, enabled its sellers to collaborate with buyers with a customized online value estimation tool. Using this application, sellers enter information about their buyers' shipping routes and frequencies, and quickly develop quantified estimates of value for improving inventory costs and time to market through more predictable shipping schedules and other factors. In collaboration with Maersk Line sellers, customers can try different scenarios and assumptions to arrive jointly at value estimates that are both believable and compelling.

As illustrated in Figure 6.1, online value calculation tools like VisualizeROI, SharkFinesse, and ROI4Sales are designed to develop persuasive cases in collaboration with buyers. Not only can these online tools encourage buyer-seller collaboration in pursuit of mutually agreed-upon estimates of value, but they are easy to use and graphically compelling. Further, the results can be shared by the buyer with other people in the organization, with full visibility to the seller. Value Drivers encourage buyers or committees to use these tools to engage in what-if analysis, so that the value estimation model becomes their own.

At SPI, we have created value models in conjunction with VisualizeROI, and share them on our website. We use these models in collaboration with our customers to determine mutually the value of improved hiring and sales productivity initiatives, as shown in Figure 6.1. (Readers are encouraged to go online and experiment with these models at www.spisales.com.)

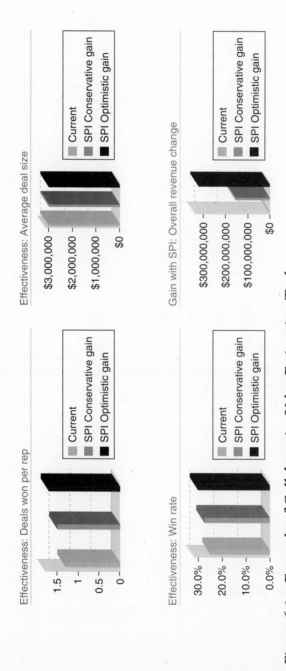

Figure 6.1 Example of Collaborative Value Estimation Tool

SPI uses VisualizeROI technology to collaborate with buyers and develop clear illustrations of the potential value of solutions.

Maximizing Organizational Value

Value is gained not only by addressing a single individual's problem or opportunity, but by also helping any related problem or opportunity managed by other people in that person's organization. Without a collaborative value estimation tool, many sellers make the mistake of focusing on the scope of an individual buyer, and not on the full impact that a solution could have on the buyer's entire organization.

Organizations are interdependent. Therefore, the organizational value of a solution is cumulative—the more people impacted, the larger the value to be received. It is imperative that the Value Driver look across the buyer organization to find all potential value. By examining the impact of a solution on all interdependent people in a buyer organization, a seller can develop a more complete estimate of value for the buyer, and establish a compelling reason to act.

Other Uses of Value Estimation

Value estimation provides sellers with several other important advantages that help them to sell more effectively.

Leverage   Sellers can offer a *quid pro quo* of quantitative estimates of value to buyers in exchange for access to other people in their organization, including those with authority and influence over the eventual purchase decision.

Differentiation   Value allows sellers to differentiate themselves. Very few sellers focus on value with their buyers. By doing so, sellers demonstrate situational fluency.

Progress   A mutually agreed-upon estimation of value is an indicator of progress with Buyer 2.0—it is a verifiable outcome that shows alignment. It provides evidence for both buyer and seller that there is a compelling reason to act.

Using a Collaboration Plan—A Buyer Alignment and Risk Mitigation Strategy

Agreement on the quantitative value of a proposed solution, by itself, may not be enough to convince Buyer 2.0 to make a buying decision. Buyers' high aversion to risk also compels them to demand proof of the viability of proposed solutions.

Buyers would not need sellers at all, if they could prove to themselves that a solution would solve a problem or capitalize on an opportunity. If they could feel assured that a capability would deliver the value expected, they would simply make the buying decision. In fact, for products they view as a commodity, Buyer 2.0 often completes transactions without sellers. For example, buyers can now make online purchases for airline tickets, hotel reservations, automobiles, clothes, books, and other commodities without the help of a seller. This trend will only grow over time as the Millennials become the largest sector of the workforce and technology advancements make the user experience for buying online easier.

For purchases of more strategic solutions, however, buyers conduct their own research to understand the "what"—the capabilities they need. The details of the "how"—the way a solution would deliver value—typically require more investigation. For this, they need a Value Driver to show proof of capabilities, as well as the time frame associated with achieving the desired results within their organization. The Value Driver persona utilizes a tool, the Collaboration Plan, to achieve this. (See Figure 6.2.)

Alignment with Buyer 2.0 should occur both procedurally and behaviorally. The Collaboration Plan serves to align buyers and sellers by identifying the procedural steps in a buying process. It is designed

Event	Week of	Responsible	Resources	Go/no go	Billable
Phone interview with John Watkins (CIO)	Feb. 14	ABC/TGI			
Phone interview with Donna Moore (COO)	Feb. 14	ABC/TGI			
Summarize findings to management team and agree on initial value estimation	Feb. 21	ABC/TGI		*	
Agree on initial value estimation	Feb. 28	ABC		*	
Perform detailed survey of current systems 2 days	March 4	ABC			Yes
Present preliminary solution design	March 11	ABC		*	
Implementation plan approval	March 18	TGI		*	
Refine final value estimation	March 18	ABC/TGI		*	
Agree on project success criteria	March 18	ABC/TGI			
Review license agreement with legal	March 18	ABC			
Gain legal approval (T&Cs)	March 18	TGI		*	
Visit corporate HQ	April 4	ABC			
Preproposal for approval	April 18	ABC			
Present proposal for approval	April 25	ABC		*	
Kickoff and finalize success criteria	May 10	ABC/TGI			
Measure success criteria	Ongoing	TGI			

*Mutual decision to proceed

Figure 6.2   Example of a Collaboration Plan

to clarify all the procedural aspects that a buyer needs to complete to make a buying decision. From a behavioral perspective, the Collaboration Plan also serves to align with the buyer's concerns and their shifts over time—for example, from determining needs to evaluating solutions to mitigating risk—and what is important to the buyer at various stages of the buying process.

For more transactional sales of smaller or limited solutions, the Collaboration Plan may simply be a short list of recommended actions by the buyer and seller organizations, with responsibilities and suggested dates for each action. For more strategic or enterprise-wide solutions, the Collaboration Plan will require a more comprehensive list of buyer and seller actions, resources, and anticipated dates for completion.

Structure of the Collaboration Plan

A Collaboration Plan can be organized in a variety of ways. We suggest it be submitted as a summary project plan. Elements could include:

- *Events*—lists activities in a sequence of interdependent activities.
- *Week*—gives suggested dates for each event. If dates are missed, the seller should negotiate new time lines and send out an amended plan.
- *Responsibility*—designates who is responsible for a given activity.
- *Resources*—lists specific people in either the buyer's organization, the seller's, or both who have an active interest in or contribution to the success of a particular activity in the plan. This ensures that they are included in the collaboration process and are given access to the collaborative portal.
- *Go/no go*—is a powerful qualifier because it requires that a decision be made about whether to proceed further in the plan. The purpose of the plan is to manage shared progress of a buyer and seller toward a mutually agreed-upon decision, whether that decision is to buy or to part ways.
- *Billable*—is optional and may not be applicable in all cases. However, this can imply to the buyer that your activities or services are valuable. Any billable item may be negotiable, but it's hard to negotiate it if it isn't first in the plan.

Activities in a Collaboration Plan

Regardless of the length or brevity of any Collaboration Plan, it should include recommended actions for addressing:

- *Operational risk issues*—proving the viability and applicability of a proposed solution to address the identified problem or opportunity.

- *Transitional risk issues*—identifying and planning for installation, implementation, and conversion requirements.

- *Financial risk issues*—arriving at a mutually agreed-upon statement of value and return on investment, and identifying and tracking the desired business results for the buyer.

- *Buying process issues*—including legal, administrative, technical, and purchasing department reviews, and required approvals by managerial or executive decision makers.

A Collaboration Plan also addresses the seller's risks, in addition to the buyer's. The seller can include actions to secure approvals from financial, legal, administrative, and procurement resources, if required. Approvals from ranking decision makers with influence and authority should also be incorporated, if needed.

However, the Collaboration Plan is not a just plan to sell, ending with a signature on an agreement. It is a jointly agreed-upon series of events for charting a course through evaluation all the way to successful business results for the buyer. The Collaboration Plan should be built to serve the mutual interests of both the buyer and the seller, by making the entire interaction open and transparent.

The Myth of Control

Unlike some popular sales theories, the philosophy of *The Collaborative Sale* is not to control the buyer. This kind of thinking is a throwback to selling practices based on Buyer 1.0 behavior. In our previous book, *The New Solution Selling*, we document this kind of control-focused approach with buyers. However, Buyer 2.0 is an empowered buyer, reluctant to give up control of the buying process. Our understanding of buyer behavior has led us to mutual collaboration as the only reasonable approach. The intent of *The Collaborative Sale* is to help sellers work in conjunction and alignment with buyers, not to control them. The Collaboration Plan is one way to demonstrate this to Buyer 2.0.

When offering a Collaboration Plan to a buyer, the preferred outcome is to have the buyer make changes and additions to it. If the buyer changes the plan, then that buyer owns the plan. A buyer who ignores a Collaboration Plan proffered by a seller, or who responds only with perfunctory acquiescence, is not really committing to joint exploration of a potential solution. A buyer who amends and improves a draft Collaboration Plan in conjunction with a seller is showing willingness to work actively together.

For this reason, mutual agreement on a Collaboration Plan is another important indicator of alignment with Buyer 2.0, and is a verifiable outcome that indicates positive progress. It is proof to both the buyer and the seller that the buyer's concerns about operational, transitional, and financial risk will be addressed—and if they are not, then the parties will disengage by mutual agreement.

Create an Online Collaboration Site

In order to encourage active collaboration with the buyer, we suggest that selling organizations create an online collaboration site—a virtual location where all information exchanged between the buyer and the seller is jointly accessible for review and edits (see Figure 6.3). This concept facilitates the essence of the Collaborative Sale, where the goal is to achieve total transparency between buyers and sellers.

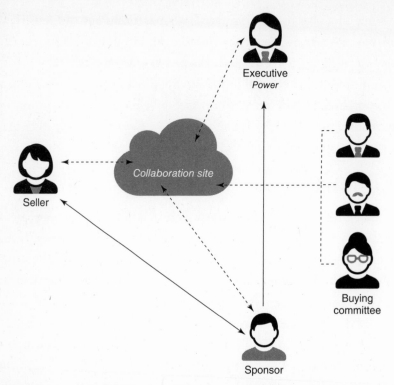

Figure 6.3   Collaboration with Multiple Stakeholders

A collaboration site enables sellers to connect with the entire buying committee, and to gain at least indirect access to everyone involved, with complete visibility as to who is accessing resources and how they are participating in the collaborative effort.

For example, to promote the mutual development of and agreement on elements of a Collaboration Plan, the seller can offer it on a secure online resource—a file-sharing facility such as Dropbox, a Microsoft SharePoint site, a secure wiki site, or a dedicated customer portal. Buyers can use this facility to add their own content, reference and forward useful resources to other people in their organization, and amend or update the Collaboration Plan as required.

One of the challenges that sellers have faced for many years is how to engage multiple people involved within a company or on a buying committee. Sellers are often blocked from having access to everyone involved in a buying decision. The Collaboration Plan, along with a collaborative portal or exchange site, provides a vehicle for everyone involved within a company to participate in the interaction taking place. Using this facility, sellers have complete visibility as to who is participating and to what degree, providing indirect access, at least, to buyer stakeholders.

Collaborating to Close

A positive result of selling collaboratively, for both buyer and seller, is that an aggressive close is usually unnecessary to secure the business. By working together through the Collaboration Plan, both buyer and seller have visibility on every aspect of the process. The selling effort is completely transparent to the buyer. Both parties know the next step toward realization of the value of the solution. Further, if the Collaboration Plan is well constructed, it will address the buyer's concerns about operational, transitional, and financial risk. Both the buyer and seller will know when it is time to make a buying decision, and the buyer will be prepared to do so.

If a buyer uses a formalized procurement process or purchasing department, that function should be included in the Collaboration Plan. Regardless of the party with whom the seller will conduct final negotiations, the seller should be well prepared after working through the actions of the plan. The seller will have a mutually agreed-upon estimate of value, clearly defined business results, and proof of alignment on the operational, transitional, and financial aspects of the solution. Armed with this knowledge, a seller is in a good position to take confident and clearly articulated positions in a final negotiation, and to make concessionary exchanges of commensurate value, if required.

Another fortuitous by-product of a Collaboration Plan is that it improves the predictability of revenues from sales opportunities. Since it is a series of steps agreed upon by both a seller and a buyer, with clear verifiable outcomes that demonstrate alignment throughout, the

Collaboration Plan identifies close dates with a high degree of accuracy. This greatly improves visibility on progress in the opportunity, and provides the seller with more confidence in anticipated buying decision dates. Managers can use this to forecast future revenues with much more certainty.

Enabling the Value Driver Persona

The Value Driver persona enables a seller to:

- Understand and position value throughout the buying process. That is, the seller leads with, sells with, and closes with value.

- Collaborate with buyers so that the discovery and confirmation of value are jointly determined.

- Use value to build a compelling business reason to act.

- Use a Collaboration Plan to influence the buying cycle and mitigate risk.

The keys to making the Value Driver persona successful are twofold. First, the seller must develop the core competency of situational fluency. Second, the organization must provide support, including the development of online collaborative tools such as a collaboration portal and interactive value estimation tools for both the web and individual sellers.

The Maersk Line story is a very good example of how to embrace the Value Driver persona at both the organizational and seller levels. Maersk Line began with a corporate initiative to sell the value of its capabilities in new ways. The company then enabled its sellers to execute the Value Driver persona, with appropriate situational fluency training and interactive online tools. The result: $111 million in new revenue, and a 350 percent return on the investment within the first year.

Value Driver Competencies

In order to successfully execute the actions needed to fulfill the Value Driver persona, a seller must possess the following essential characteristics, knowledge, skills, and abilities:

- *Situational knowledge*—understands the buyer's industry, job roles, areas of responsibility, and common business issues.

- *Capability knowledge*—understands product and service solutions, and how they address customer business issues or capitalize on potential opportunities.

- *Value identification and articulation*—determines scope and impact of buyer problems or potential opportunities; identifies, quantifies, and communicates the tangible results of proposed solutions; can identify or create compelling reasons to act based on value.

- *Financial acumen*—understands buyers' financial statements, key performance measures, and how their decisions will affect value creation.

- *Risk management skills*—can relate to and understand buyers' risks at both the individual level and the organizational level; can take appropriate actions to mitigate buyer risks.

- *Technical skills*—is able to use appropriate technology to operate business impact and value analysis estimation tools, such as online collaborative value calculators and specialized Excel worksheets.

- *Customer focus*—keeps the customer foremost in mind; advocates for the customer's best interests; can anticipate

(continued)

potential solution transition and implementation issues for specific customers and recommend appropriate actions and resources to address those issues.

- *Communication skills*—has ability to express points of view clearly, both orally and in written form.

The Story (Continued)

Jon had been collaborating with the insurance broker on a Visualize-ROI online value estimation. They were making progress, thanks to an analyst report Jon had discovered that stated that the broker's firm reported profits down 10 percent over the past two years while firms with similar portfolios were up 7 percent in the same time frame. No amount of further research resolved the mystery behind the 17 percent difference, but the broker willingly admitted to Jon that the brokerage's actuaries had priced a risk pool inaccurately and it had cost the firm dearly. A $20 million value model had become $35 million and a five-year return on investment (ROI) was close to 23 percent.

Jon dialed both the CEO and Nancy after meeting with the broker to review the results of the demo meeting he'd just finished using data from the broker. "It was terrific before it became problematic," he said from his rental car.

"This new guy they'd just hired to do some organizational development work started flexing his muscles. It was the first time I'd met him. He carried on about teaching people the new system and how it would affect work flows. He was a jerk."

Nancy asked, "What about your sponsor? How'd he react?"

"He texted me in the meeting to say that he knew a politician when he saw one; not to worry. We're going to collaborate with the guy on a new implementation schedule to overcome those transitional issues."

"When they develop or change your proposed plan, they own it," said Nancy. "This sounds promising, Jon, but be sure to find a way to let the new guy shine as a result of hiring us. Let's show him how this could be an early career win with his company, and you'll have a friend for life."

Later, Jon logged in to the online customer portal site and opened the Collaboration Plan. He amended the Event, Responsible, and Resources columns in the plan he had drafted with the broker before that meeting. Over the next two days, the two iterated the plan, and then scheduled a conference call with the new manager who had raised objections in the demo. Jon knew if he could get him to collaborate on their plan, he could win this business.

Part III
Making the Collaborative Sale a Reality

7 Establishing a Dynamic Sales Process

I n 2012, a CSO Insights survey of more than 1,400 sales executives found that nearly nine out of every 10 organizations that implement a defined sales process report significant improvements in business performance.[1]

One of our clients, Microsoft, was able to confirm and quantify the value of its sales process implementation. To accomplish this, it established a control group of sellers who utilized the Microsoft Solution Selling Process, while all other sellers did not. They then compared sellers' performance results for each group over two years.[2] See Figure 7.1 for results from the comparative study.

The performance of sellers utilizing the Microsoft Solution Selling Process was far superior to the worldwide average of sellers not using

---

[1] *Sales Performance Optimization Report*, CSO Insights, 2012. Also at www .csoinsights.com.
[2] *Microsoft Internal Study*, Summer 2006. Comparative analysis of Microsoft Solution Sales Process on seller performance, based on worldwide customer satisfaction surveys and internal interviews. Published with permission of Microsoft Corporation, Redmond, Washington.

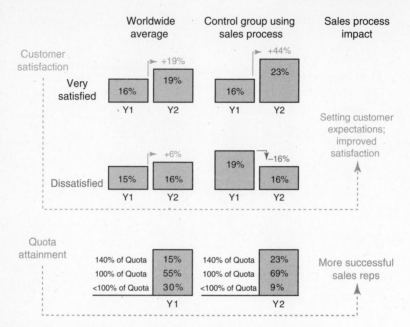

Figure 7.1   Microsoft Solution Sales Process Results
Source: Microsoft Internal Study, Summer 2006, Microsoft
Corporation, Redmond, Washington. Published with permission of
Microsoft.

the sales process. In particular, sellers using the sales process produced
much better customer satisfaction ratings. Why? Those sellers were better at setting and managing customer expectations. They accomplished
this through improved conversations; they had learned how to diagnose buyer problems and create visions of solutions that were realistic.

In addition to improved customer satisfaction, those who used the
sales process realized improvements in quota attainment as well. The
most significant difference was in the percentage of sellers achieving
their quotas. The number of sellers using the Microsoft Solution
Selling Process who achieved or exceeded their quotas increased
significantly.

As Figure 7.2 indicates, CSO Insights also discovered a correlation between the level of sales process implemented (described as

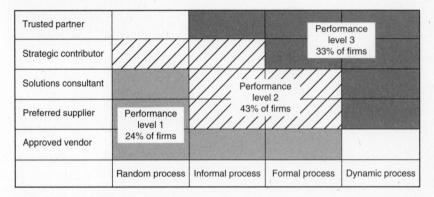

	Random process	Informal process	Formal process	Dynamic process
Trusted partner				
Strategic contributor			Performance level 3 33% of firms	
Solutions consultant		Performance level 2 43% of firms		
Preferred supplier	Performance level 1 24% of firms			
Approved vendor				

Figure 7.2 Relationship of Sales Process Maturity and Level of Relationship

Source: Sales Performance Optimization Report, CSO Insights, 2012.
www.csoinsights.com. Chart reproduced with permission of CSO
Insights.

random, informal, formal, and dynamic) and the levels of customer
relationship (categorized as approved vendor, preferred supplier,
solutions consultant, strategic contributor, and trusted partner). In
short, the more mature the sales process definition, the higher the
general level of customer relationship.

Why do some sellers achieve trusted partner status with buyers,
while others can attain only lower relationship levels? In Figure 7.3,
we define five different levels of customer relationship. We have
observed that most sellers' opinions of how their customers view
them are higher than their customers' actual opinions. In addition,
sellers' actual relationship level will likely vary with different customers. The goal, however, is to strive for the highest level—trusted
partner.

The key to gaining higher levels of buyer relationship is the seller's
situational fluency. The better sellers develop their situational and
capability knowledge along with their people skills, selling skills, and
collaborative attitude, the more insightful and valuable will be the

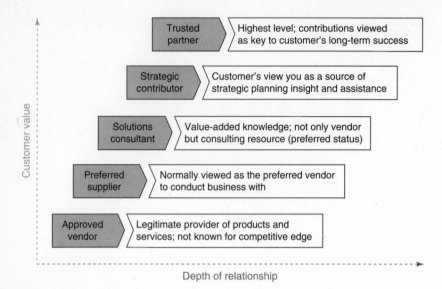

Figure 7.3   Moving Up the Relationship Staircase

conversations that they can have with buyers, and therefore the higher the level of relationship they can achieve.

The combination of sales process and customer relationship translates into significantly better sales performance. The top tier of sales organizations—what CSO Insights calls Level 3, attained by one-third of the survey respondents—operate with the highest levels of both sales process and buyer relationship. They report the best aggregate average results for:

- Sales team goal attainment
- Individual sales goal attainment
- Forecast accuracy
- Sales staff turnover reduction
- Adoption and usage of customer relationship management (CRM)[3]

---

[3] *Sales Performance Optimization Report,* CSO Insights, 2012. Also at www.csoinsights.com.

Some observers of sales methodology argue that since Buyer 2.0 engages with sellers later in their buying process, the value of a defined sales process is now greatly diminished. However, this belief does not hold up against research findings. The Microsoft results and the CSO Insights studies prove that implementing a defined sales process is strongly correlated to customer satisfaction and relationship, and to improved business results.

The reason for this is that Buyer 2.0 does not make purchase decisions randomly. Today buyers use a rational sequence of events to identify business issues or opportunities, define corresponding needs and requirements, evaluate alternatives, and assess the risks of making a decision. Buyer 2.0 moves through the psychological phases of evaluation and decision in a fairly predictable and consistent way. A defined sales process that aligns with Buyer 2.0's behavior enables sellers to collaborate in harmony with buyers' concerns, and help them to a buying decision.

In previous chapters, we defined the three personae needed to engage collaboratively with Buyer 2.0—the Micro-Marketer, the Visualizer, and the Value Driver. In order to assume the right persona at the right time, sellers need to have some context based on where a buyer is in the buying process. A dynamic sales process, one that aligns with a variety of buying scenarios, helps sellers to understand this context and therefore what persona they should assume to engage effectively with Buyer 2.0. This is why the three personae of *The Collaborative Sale* work so well, as they enable sellers to align with the concerns of Buyer 2.0 as they progress through the buying phases.

The question is not whether a sales process provides value, but rather: does a sales process look different today, given the changes in buyer behavior? We have found that in order to help sellers engage more collaboratively with buyers, an evolution of sales process is needed. A more *dynamic* sales process is required to align with Buyer 2.0.

Buyer-Aligned Sales Process

A *process* is a systematic series of actions, or a series of defined, repeatable steps, intended to achieve a reliable result. When followed, these steps can lead consistently to predictable outcomes.

Our automobiles, for example, are assembled using manufacturing processes, as are our clothes, our homes, and even the foods we eat. Each relies on defined processes to ensure quality and consistency. Imagine what our automobiles might look like if they were constructed haphazardly, without a defined manufacturing process, and how unsafe and unreliable they would be. Similarly, a sales effort without any direction or definition too often leads to unfavorable results—or increasingly, to no result at all.

A buyer-aligned sales process, however, is different from other kinds of processes in one important way. While a good selling process includes recommendations for seller actions and best practices, progress and success are measured by the observed *verifiable outcomes*, not by the activities executed. The reason for this is that verifiable outcomes demonstrate validations of human behavior. Sales process is not an exact science.

A verifiable outcome is a behavior that shows the degree of alignment between a buyer and the seller—and those behaviors are always executed by the buyer, not the seller. This aspect is what makes this a buyer-aligned sales process, not just a selling process—and this distinction is vital for enabling sellers to collaborate successfully with Buyer 2.0.

Verifiable outcomes can be captured as evidence of progress with a buyer. For example, after an initial meeting with a buyer, a seller can summarize the results of that conversation in an e-mail, sent back to the buyer. The verifiable outcome is how that buyer reacts to that message. Does the buyer confirm the conclusions of the seller and agree to next steps? Or does the buyer amend or change those conclusions? Or does the buyer not react at all? The observed behavior tells the seller the degree to which he or she is aligning with a buyer.

Dynamic Sales Process

Buyer 2.0 is changing the face of sales process in such a way that a single picture or simple linear view no longer represents what is needed. Driving the need for process flexibility is how buyers now engage sellers. For example, a traditional sales process step covering activities for initial discovery will not be applicable for every opportunity with Buyer 2.0, who generally engages sellers later in the buying process. Today, a sales process must reflect multiple buying scenarios, with different points of initial engagement with Buyer 2.0, as shown in Figure 7.4.

A "one size fits all" sales process is no longer applicable to engaging with Buyer 2.0. Today, sales organizations use many different go-to-market models to connect with buyers. A sales process defined for an inside sales team will be different from one for a direct or channel sales team. Within each model, there can be multiple variations of sales process dependent on the buyers served, complexity of the solution sold, and typical length of the buying process, as illustrated in Figure 7.5.

For example, one of our clients, Emerson Process Management, offers individual products, such as an advanced pump for a manufacturing line, and also larger strategic solutions, such as fully integrated plant control systems. The individual product sale tends to be shorter, is focused on fewer people in the evaluation process, and is more tactical than the strategic solution sale, which tends to be longer with a more rigorous evaluation, a larger group of evaluators, and more complex requirements.

Emerson Process Management has therefore defined two types of buyer-aligned sales processes, one for transactional sales and another

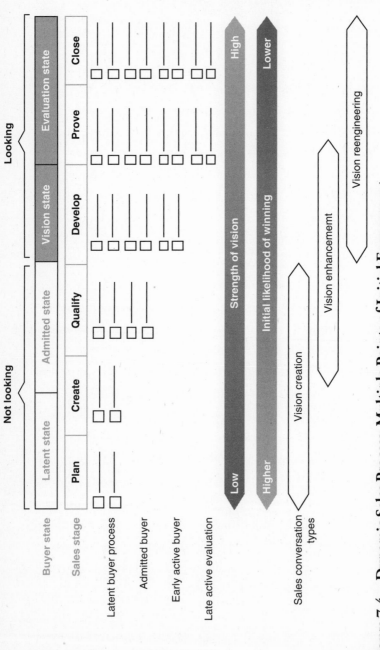

Figure 7.4 Dynamic Sales Process: Multiple Points of Initial Engagement

The actual number and names of sales stages may vary, depending on the nature of the buyer constituencies served and relevant solutions sold. Recommended seller actions for different points of initial buyer engagement are critical for an effective dynamic sales process definition.

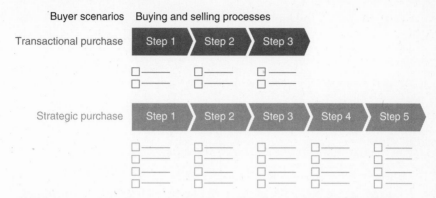

Figure 7.5   One Size Does Not Fit All: Processes for Multiple Buying Scenarios

for more strategic sales, to reflect these typical kinds of buyers. Sellers use either type of process as a guide, depending on the situation and what is most appropriate to that particular opportunity.

Optimally, buyer-aligned sales processes should be designed to cover the most typical buying scenarios, but not every conceivable type. A good rule of thumb is to develop process definitions that ensure alignment for the majority of typical buyer scenarios—more is good, but absolute perfection is not required. Any situations that do not align perfectly with defined processes are, by definition, exceptions, and should be managed accordingly. In fact, defining dynamic buyer-aligned sales processes makes the principle of "management by exception" a clear decision, instead of an arbitrary or subjective one.

Automating Dynamic Sales Processes

While a diversity of sales process definitions may seem overwhelming or complex, it can be made simple by providing sellers with a playbook—a guide for best practices for each of the typical sales situations they encounter. A playbook provides sellers with advice for effective activities, tools, and conversations targeted to each scenario.

In addition, providing a playbook that covers multiple sales processes using an automated tool within a CRM system can make it easier for sellers to select and apply the most appropriate option for the particular scenario they are encountering with a buyer.

An application platform that supports development of a playbook of dynamic sales processes for use in different sales scenarios can help sellers to align with Buyer 2.0 more accurately, and therefore, execute the right actions that will be of most benefit to both the buyer and the seller. (See Figure 7.6.) We explore the implementation of automated playbooks in more detail in Chapter 9.

Expanding the View of Sales Process

It is not enough simply to have a sales process. The sales process's philosophical underpinnings must be based on collaboratively solving customer problems—it must be customer focused and solution based. To be a little more granular, this means it is not just about "what to do"; the process needs to be supported with methodologies covering "how to do it" as well.

The sales process definition should include all end-to-end actions that lead to increased performance. Many people think of sales process only in the context of sales execution—the direct interaction with a buyer focused on a specific sales opportunity—but this is too limited a view. An effective sales process definition should also include relevant sales planning steps and methodologies.

Planning methodologies at the channel, territory, account, and opportunity levels are typically conducted on a periodic basis—every year, quarter, month, or week, depending on the customary management review cycle of a particular business. These methodologies support and integrate with the sales execution process at the opportunity level, which focuses on day-to-day selling activities with buyers.

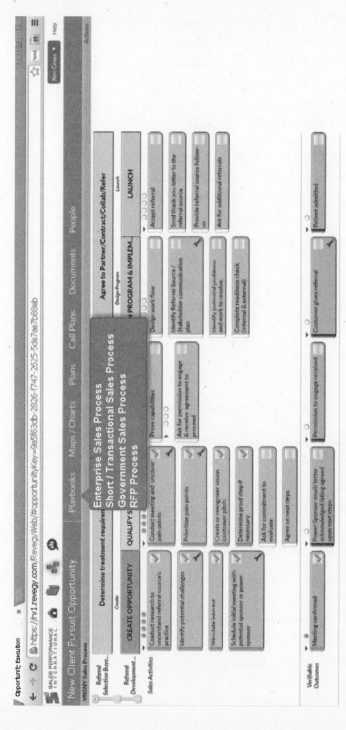

Figure 7.6 Dynamic Sales Process Playbooks

This is an example of an automated dynamic sales process and the user interface for a seller using the Revegy platform within a CRM system. This platform supports multiple playbooks that align with the types of buyer with whom a seller may engage. It allows the seller to use the optimum sales process for each buyer scenario.

Collaboration is essential in most supporting planning methodologies. For example, account planning ideally should be conducted jointly with the customer and also involve relevant sales team and customer support resources. Collaboration goes beyond opportunity management and sales execution, and should be a part of any sales methodology utilized.

Each of the sales planning methods could be a stand-alone process; they are their own processes. We are not defining planning methodologies in detail within this book, as we are focusing primarily on the process of sales execution and alignment with Buyer 2.0. However, planning methodologies can and should be supported in conjunction with sales execution on a common automation platform, which makes integration and user compliance easier. An automated platform can help to integrate sales methodologies seamlessly to ensure quality completion of both planning and sales execution tasks. (See Figure 7.7.)

Sales Process Enables Management and Marketing

Sellers are not the only beneficiaries of defined standards for a dynamic buyer-aligned sales process. Marketing can use playbooks to equip and enable sellers to diagnose buyer situations, position appropriate solutions, and manage concerns about risk. Process definitions and associated playbooks also provide standards for first-line sales managers and executives for use in coaching and sales forecasting.

With playbook definitions, marketing professionals can understand what sellers need to help them align with buyers better—the messages, enabling tools, and collateral materials that would be of the most help in different buyer scenarios. Further, a dynamic sales process provides common standards for developing marketing messages that are most compatible within the context of a sales process. In our previous book, *The Solution-Centric Organization*, we described how

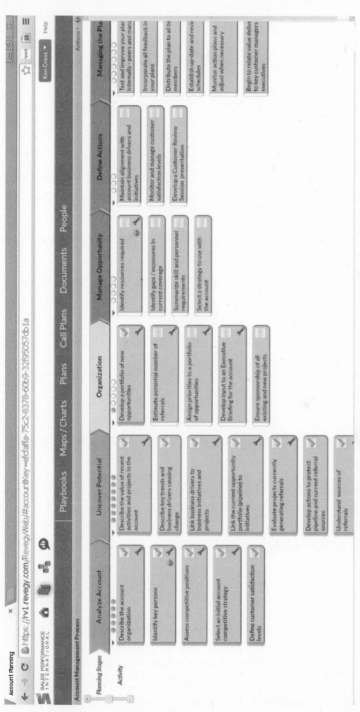

Figure 7.7 Example of an Automated Account Planning Methodology

This is an example of a user interface screen for an account planning process using the Revegy platform. By using a common platform for planning and sales execution methodology support, integration and user compliance are easier to accomplish.

141

sales and marketing can be aligned to work together seamlessly.[4] Definition of a dynamic sales process is the common ground upon which sales and marketing can integrate their efforts.

Executives can also use dynamic sales processes to tabulate forecasts of future business, based on the cumulative likelihood of winning opportunities. Using a dynamic sales process, the likelihood of winning can be based on the degree of alignment with buyers, the progression through the buying process, and the expected date of a buyer decision, all proven by observed verifiable outcomes. Using objective criteria, the accuracy of dynamic sales process forecasts will be higher than those derived from compiled subjective estimates from sales managers.

With a definition of "what good looks like" in dynamic sales processes, managers can evaluate the status of opportunities more accurately, assess the quality of each opportunity, and coach sellers to an agreed-upon standard of excellence. Without a definition of sales process, managers have few benchmarks to compare an opportunity against, making it difficult if not impossible to ascertain its true status, or to determine the optimal actions a seller should apply. In the next chapter, we further explore the use of sales process to coach sellers in the Collaborative Sale.

---

[4]Keith M. Eades and Robert E. Kear, *The Solution-Centric Organization* (New York: McGraw-Hill, 2006).

8 Coaching the Collaborative Sale

Exceptional performance in any endeavor doesn't happen by accident. Even world-class athletes need coaches and motivational assistance to develop their natural talents and reach their maximum potential. Artists need teachers and mentors to develop the essential skills of their craft. Sellers are no different from any other professional in this regard.

How often have you seen sales organizations make major investments in sales performance improvement initiatives (training, process, or automation), only to see sales teams produce less than expected results? Taking this a level deeper, why are many of these initiatives successful within one region or division but not in others?

It's probably not the economy or market conditions, because it's the same for everyone. It's probably not the sellers or the hiring model, because they were assessed and hired based on the same hiring and competency model. And it's certainly not because of the training and enablement programs they have been through; everyone has been given the same training and tools.

The difference is due to the leadership, sales management, and coaching they've received. The key to achieving consistent sales results is effective and systematic coaching along with both internal and external motivation.

Sales managers can help their teams accelerate the time to results by systematic coaching and by embracing and mastering collaborative selling methods. Unfortunately, not all sales managers really know what it means to be an effective coach and mentor. Most simply dispense advice to their sellers based on what they would have done, or how they used to handle different situations when they were sellers.

Some of this advice might be good, but as Buyer 2.0 behavior becomes the norm, some formerly effective ways of engaging with buyers may no longer work very well. In fact, they may be based on old assumptions that are now dead wrong.

The best sales managers are those who coach sellers against an agreed-upon standard of excellence. They understand that their role is not simply to recant how they used to sell, but rather to help sellers see how they can meet or exceed the standard by executing the right behaviors, at the right times, with the right people. The principles of *The Collaborative Sale* are the standards of sales behavior required to engage successfully with Buyer 2.0.

If you are a sales manager, coaching consistency is vital to the successful development of your sellers. It is also what sellers want from their managers. By using the principles of *The Collaborative Sale* as consistent standards of sales excellence, managers can coach more effectively, and sellers will understand better what they need to do to perform well. Consistent coaching, continuous learning, and regular reinforcement are the keys to effective sales leadership and improved sales team results.

Sales Management Cadence

Coaching consistency begins with establishing commonly understood sales processes, and then a regular cadence for inspection of sales

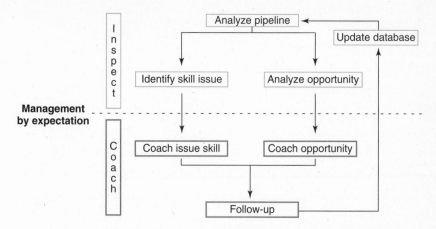

Figure 8.1   Sales Management Inspection and Coaching Cycle

activity and results. This cadence will vary according to each company's standards for business reporting. For many of our clients, first-line sales managers conduct a weekly inspection of seller performance, but for those with shorter average selling times, this review might be daily or even more frequent.

Regardless of the frequency established for routine inspection and review, effective sales management includes a systematic and consistent cycle of inspection and coaching, as shown in Figure 8.1.

Systematic Inspection

In the inspect phase, sales managers first analyze their teams' pipeline content and quality. Are they sufficient to attain individual and team sales goals? Are opportunities progressing as expected, or are any of them stalled? Are there enough new opportunities entering the pipeline? The findings of these lines of inquiry determine if there are any exceptional cases that require deeper review, and if any coaching must take place at the opportunity or selling skills level, or both. The manager can then schedule appropriate follow-up reviews with sellers, and can update the business system of record, ideally a customer relationship management (CRM) platform.

The shape of a seller's sales pipeline is an indicator of collaborative selling skill issues. If there is an insufficient number or value of opportunities in the pipeline to achieve sales goals, then that is an indication that the seller may not be executing the Micro-Marketer persona effectively. The seller may need help with targeting, messaging, and nurturing conversations with Buyer 2.0, or may not be recognizing potential opportunities as they emerge from those conversations. Sellers may not be using social media effectively to reach potential buyers. They may lack the situational fluency to understand how to help targeted buyers with problems or potential opportunities, and may be in need of further training and education.

If opportunities in the pipeline are stalling in the middle stages of a sales process, then the seller is probably not executing the Visualizer persona effectively. He or she may need help in executing consultative sales conversations to create, enhance, or reengineer buyers' visions.

If opportunities in the pipeline appear to be stalling in later stages, then the seller is probably not executing the Value Driver persona well. Sellers may need help in collaborating with buyers to build compelling estimates of value for the envisioned solution. They may be forgetting some aspect of a Collaboration Plan that would help the buyer to mitigate the perception of risk, and make it easier to go forward with the purchase decision.

Sales managers can quickly inspect the quality of opportunities in the pipeline by observing the verifiable outcomes for each stage in a buyer-aligned sales process. For example, if a seller says that the buyer has agreed to a mutually determined vision of a solution, but there is no verifiable outcome, then something is amiss. By assessing the opportunities in the pipeline, managers can better project what they are likely to attain in the future—in both the short term and the long term. As a result, forecasts of future revenue can be much more accurate, since they are then based on objective, observable buyer behavior, instead of subjective estimates.

Management by exception is made possible by the use of objective, verifiable outcomes, defined in buyer-aligned dynamic sales processes. Any opportunity that complies with the standards of *The Collaborative Sale*—that is, it is progressing according to expectations, with good-quality, verifiable outcomes from buyers—is simply noted for future review. No deeper inspection is required of opportunities that are in compliance with agreed-upon standards. However, any opportunity that does not fully comply with agreed-upon standards is easily identified for deeper examination and specific coaching.

Coaching

Just like collaborating with buyers, sales coaching is about aligning with sellers to come to a mutually agreed vision of a better future state—one in which the seller is successful. To enable this alignment, a consistent standard for coaching conversations helps both the manager and the seller to engage in a productive discussion and come to that vision together.

After completing the diagnosis of a seller's pipeline and opportunities, a sales manager should then prepare in advance for the coaching conversation with a seller. The key points of the intended conversation should include:

- **G**—Specific **gaps** identified between pipeline value, selling skills, or specific opportunity issues and collaborative selling behavior standards and expectations
- **R**—Possible **reasons** for identified gaps
- **A**—**Actions** needed to close the identified gaps
- **F**—**Follow-up** steps and timing

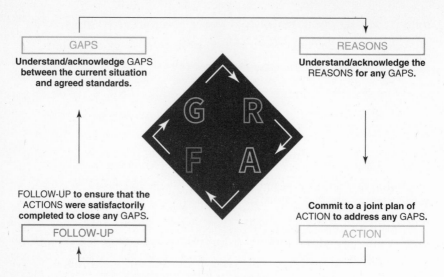

Figure 8.2   The GRAF Coaching Model

This approach, illustrated in Figure 8.2 and abbreviated as GRAF, is the basis of every good sales coaching conversation. It is a straightforward discussion based on observed facts and objective standards. It is designed to empower sellers—not to criticize them—with clear actions for improvement toward absolute mastery of collaborative selling and, more important, toward improved performance and the rewards that go with it.

Coaching to Win Opportunities   Sales managers can be an invaluable resource for helping sellers figure out how to win sales opportunities—or more importantly, when to qualify out. The decision to walk away from an opportunity is difficult for most sellers. The reason that sellers are reluctant to walk away from unqualified business is simple: they usually don't have enough opportunities in their current pipelines.

One way to determine if further engagement with a potential buyer is warranted is to use objective criteria for assessing the sales opportunity. We call these criteria the Sales Success Formula, and it consists of six components:

$$P \times P \times V \times V \times C \times C = \text{Sale}$$

The components of the formula are:

- **P—Pain** (problem, critical business issue, or potential missed opportunity). Do we know what buyer pains(s) we are solving? Has the buyer admitted that there is a problem, critical business issue, or potential missed opportunity that needs to be addressed?

- **P—Power** (people with influence or authority). Do we know the people in the buyer organization with influence and authority, related to this opportunity? Can we gain access to them? Can we influence their thinking? Do they support a mutually determined vision that includes our solution?

- **V—Vision.** Do all of the stakeholders agree on a vision of a solution? Can we provide unique or highly differentiated aspects of the vision?

- **V—Value.** Have we quantified the value of the problem, critical business issue, or potential missed opportunity? Have we quantified the value of the proposed solution? Does the buyer agree that there is enough value in our solution to take action?

- **C—Collaborate.** Have we and the buyer agreed on a mutual plan for action—a Collaboration Plan? Is the buyer collaborating with us? Are we engaged actively with the buyer to help progress toward a purchase decision, in a way that minimizes or mitigates the buyer's risk?

- **C—Compelling reason to act.** Is there a time-bound event that is driving the purchase decision, beyond which bad things may happen? Are these potentially negative implications of delay acknowledged by the buyer?

In applying this formula, assign one of the following values to each criterion:

+ = All answers are known for this criterion, and they are favorable to us.

? = Answers are currently unknown for this criterion.

− = At least some answers are known for this criterion, and they are unfavorable to us.

If all criteria in the formula are positive, then the chances of winning the sale are very high. If there are any unknown factors, then the outcome is still indefinite, and your activity should focus on understanding the true nature of any uncertain criteria. If any criteria are negative, then the chances of winning the sale go virtually to zero; unless you can realistically change the value of those criteria, then you should consider qualifying out of that opportunity.

When we conduct opportunity reviews with clients, we are often surprised by how often sellers ignore aspects of this formula. It is a helpful tool for determining the strength of the sales effort in each opportunity, and for identifying specific actions that are needed in order to improve the certainty of winning—or for qualifying out.

There should be no shame in deciding to walk away from an unlikely sales opportunity. We sometimes tell our clients to think of sales opportunities as playing a poker game with multiple rounds of betting in each hand. The winner of every hand of poker is the one who either has the winning cards or is the last player remaining after all others have folded. But who comes in second place? The answer we usually get is "Nobody," but that is not really correct. The player who comes in second is the one who folded first, because that player bet the least on a bad hand. If that player looked at his or her initial cards and deduced objectively that the odds of winning were low, the player made a wise choice in folding first.

Unfortunately, too many sellers do not do this. If they find a potential sales opportunity, many continue to invest their time and company resources in hopes of winning, without ever really taking an objective measure of the chances of doing so. A sales manager using the Sales Success Formula can keep them honest, and can coach sellers to make a correct decision about when they should wisely withdraw.

Coaching Is Leverage   In major sports, coaches don't play the game—the players do. It should be the same for sellers. Unfortunately, it is far too common to see sales managers jumping into opportunities and taking charge, rather than allowing sellers to learn from doing and from coaching.

Sales managers who parachute into developing sales opportunities to close disempower their sales team, and therefore make it very difficult to engage collaboratively with Buyer 2.0. Further, one sales manager cannot be everywhere at once. The only way to maximize the performance of the entire team is to enable every seller to execute consistently to the standards of *The Collaborative Sale*.

Motivation

Why is motivation a key part of sales leadership? Aren't sellers supposed to be naturally motivated? Aren't their personal strengths supposed to include characteristics such as being driven, competitive, focused, dominant, and friendly? Why does a person like this need motivation?

In psychology, motivation is generally described as something that causes people to act. If someone is hungry, motivation is what drives them to get something to eat. This example seems very basic, and it is; after all, eating is a physical need similar to sleeping, resting, or even sex.

Motivation is more than what drives us to meet our physical needs; it is also the inner drive within us that causes us to act in a certain way or to do certain things that we are not required to do. It's why some people get up early, exercise, and run for an hour even if they don't have to. It's what drives some people to succeed whereas others fail even with the same parents, intelligence levels, and upbringing. A wise man (Keith's father) used to say when he saw a person doing something really special that they didn't have to do but simply wanted to do it, "Son, I don't know what drives that person, but whatever it is, find a way to bottle it up and we can make a fortune."

As parents, teachers, employers, or coaches, we have all seen people around us who are motivated to achieve and still others who are not. We have all experienced very talented and exceptionally intelligent people who are not motivated. So what can we do?

First, we must understand the true nature of motivation, which can be divided into two types: intrinsic (internal) motivation and extrinsic (external) motivation.

Intrinsic motivation is generally regarded as motivation that comes from or originates from the satisfaction or enjoyment of doing something—a job, a task, or something you like to do. It is also associated with the drive within the individual rather than relying on external pressures or a desire for reward. Sellers who are intrinsically motivated are more likely to engage on their own as well as work to improve their knowledge, skills, and abilities.

Extrinsic motivation generally refers to motivation that comes from the desire to attain an outcome, and it generally comes from outside of the individual. Common extrinsic motivations are rewards (e.g., money, prizes, and promotions) for demonstrating the desired behavior, and the possibility of punishment for noncompliant behavior.

If you play golf for the competition to win a trophy, it's considered extrinsic motivation. If you play golf because you enjoy the friendship and camaraderie of your friends while playing, it's considered intrinsic motivation. If a seller spends extra time doing research on a customer's problem because the seller loves knowledge, it's intrinsic motivation. If sellers do research only because they can't win the business without it, or they do the research only because their boss said, "You won't have a job anymore if you don't do this research," that's extrinsic motivation.

The reason for including this discussion in this chapter is to get sales leaders, sales managers, and sales coaches to think about motivation from a multidimensional perspective. Too often, we fall into the trap of thinking the key to driving sales results is through rewards and incentives. This isn't always the case. No doubt rewards can drive short-term performance, but in order to sustain long-term sales performance, sales managers and coaches must focus on the intrinsic motivators, not only on external motivators. You want to find a way to tap into the extra gear that drives performance.

The outcome of external motivation is often a short-term performance gain, quickly followed by a drop in motivation when the reward is achieved or the threat is gone. In contrast, if a sales manager or coach can tap into the seller's needs for competence, relatedness, and autonomy as defined by Self-Determination Theory (SDT),[1] then the result is internal motivation. These are key ingredients to motivation that will lead to sustained performance over time.

What is Self-Determination Theory all about? SDT was initially developed by Edward L. Deci and Richard M. Ryan, and has been elaborated and refined by scholars from many countries. Deci and Ryan are professors in the Department of Clinical and Social Sciences in Psychology at the University of Rochester, New York, where they direct a pre- and postdoctoral training program focused on SDT.

---

[1] Edward Deci and Richard Ryan, "Self-Determination Theory," University of Rochester Motivation Research Group. Accessed December 1, 2013, at www .selfdeterminationtheory.org.

To quote from the SDT website:

> People are centrally concerned with *motivation*—how to
> move themselves or others to act. Everywhere, parents,
> teachers, coaches, and managers struggle with how to
> motivate those that they mentor, and individuals struggle
> to find energy, mobilize effort, and persist at the tasks of
> life and work. People are often moved by external factors
> such as reward systems, grades, evaluations, or the opinions
> they fear others might have of them. Yet just as frequently,
> people are motivated from within, by interests, curiosity,
> care, or abiding values. These intrinsic motivations are not
> necessarily externally rewarded or supported, but nonethe-
> less they can sustain passions, creativity, and sustained
> efforts. The interplay between the extrinsic forces acting
> on persons and the intrinsic motives and needs inherent
> in human nature is the territory of Self-Determination
> Theory.[2]

Focus on Intrinsic Motivation

Since the outcome of external motivation is often a short-term performance gain, quickly followed by a drop, the obvious question is: what
else should we be doing? According to SDT, the answer is to satisfy the
seller's need for intrinsic motivation, including competence, relatedness, and autonomy.

- *Competence.* People need to feel valuable based on their experience
  and knowledge, including the mastery of tasks or skills. Situational
  fluency is the foundational competency required to facilitate the
  Collaborative Sale. When sales managers and coaches help sellers

---

[2]Ibid.

develop and utilize situational fluency, they are inherently supporting this aspect of intrinsic motivation.

- *Relatedness or connection.* People need to experience a sense of belonging and attachment to other people. This includes collaboration with colleagues, coworkers, and customers. The philosophy and the tools of *The Collaborative Sale* support this aspect of intrinsic motivation as well. Collaboration is the cornerstone of the approach.

- *Autonomy.* People need to feel in control of their own behaviors and goals rather than feeling they are being controlled by someone else. The three personae of *The Collaborative Sale* support this aspect of intrinsic motivation. The Micro-Marketer, the Visualizer, and the Value Driver are empowering character parts that sellers must play in selling to Buyer 2.0. Each persona supports the seller's need for autonomy and independence.

Sales managers and coaches should be happy to know that developing sellers' intrinsic motivations is not their responsibility. It is, in fact, the responsibility of every individual. However, sales managers do have a responsibility to create the supporting environment that enables internal motivation to thrive. Reliance upon external rewards does not provide lasting results. Sales managers must balance this by creating a work environment that allows sellers' intrinsic motivations—their sense of competence, connection, and autonomy—to flourish. Coaching and reinforcing the principles of *The Collaborative Sale* appeal to all of these intrinsic motivations, and can help to sustain long-term improvement in sales team results. That is the essence of effective sales leadership.

9 Implementing the Collaborative Sale

O ur instant gratification mind-set society likes immediate improvements in productivity. Many sales executives often look for
so-called silver bullets, such as a new technology, a new compensation
and reward system, a new training program, and so forth, to make an
immediate and positive improvement in their team's performance.
Unfortunately, the results of these kinds of tactical fixes are inevitably
lackluster, because they individually fail to address all obstacles to sales
growth and success.

Successful implementation of the Collaborative Sale is based on
a holistic approach, which includes people, process, methods, and
tools to enable individual sellers and entire organizations to achieve
sustainable improvement in performance, now and into the future.
This implementation approach makes it possible to accelerate time to
improved results, such as:

- *Improved customer satisfaction*, as a result of better collaboration
- *More sales revenues*, as a result of higher win rates
- *Larger opportunities*, as sellers develop broader visions of solutions
  with buyers
- *More opportunities*, as sellers learn to find and develop latent buyers

- *Better margins*, as a result of quantifying and proving value throughout the buying process—proven value that translates into lower price discounts and other concessions

In 2013, AberdeenGroup studied more than 300 global companies to learn about their deployments of sales performance improvement training.[1] They discovered that the best-performing companies not only provided training, but also supported organizational behavior change in three key areas, illustrated in Figure 9.1.

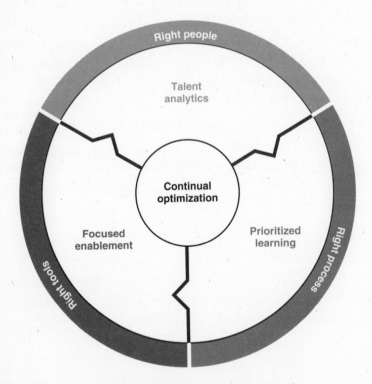

Figure 9.1   Sales Performance Optimization Cycle

---

[1] Peter Ostrow, "Sales Performance Optimization 2013: Aligning the Right People, Processes, and Tools," *Research Brief*, AberdeenGroup, February 2, 2013. Accessed December 1, 2013, at www.aberdeen.com/Aberdeen-Library/8347/RB-sales-performance-optimization.aspx.

1. *Right process.* The best-performing companies develop world-class capabilities by aligning sales process, methods, and continual learning to buyer behaviors.

2. *Right people.* They assess the specific talent requirements for their sales models and align hiring and development to those profiles.

3. *Right tools.* They enable effective, consistent application of best practices by integrating supporting tools and technologies.

We refer to the proper alignment of process, people, and tools as the Sales Performance Optimization Cycle. Each of these factors contributes to the success of the others. When all three are incorporated into an implementation plan, they maximize the adoption and consistent application of selling best practices, and thereby produce sustainable improvement in results. If any one of these factors is missing or disproportionate to the others, then the success of the sales performance improvement initiative is at risk. An effective implementation of the Collaborative Sale requires thoughtful inclusion and alignment of all three components.

Right Process: Buyer-Aligned Learning and Development

An effective learning and development strategy is an important part of implementing the Collaborative Sale, and it entails three key components, shown in Figure 9.2.

Using Dynamic Sales Processes

Sellers will need coaching and guidance in order to master the three personae of *The Collaborative Sale*. By defining dynamic buyer-aligned sales processes, you provide a standard of excellence for effective coaching and skills development. A definition of dynamic sales processes also enables the establishment of critical competencies needed to find

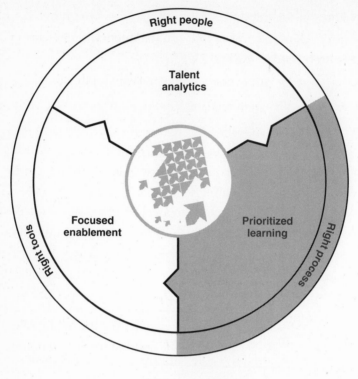

Right process

- Adapt process models to reflect buyer behavior
- Align methodology and skills training to buyer-aligned models and relevant competencies
- Treat learning as a transformative experience

Figure 9.2   Three Key Components for Right Process for the Collaborative Sale

and develop the right people. For these reasons, the first major step in successfully implementing the Collaborative Sale is conducting an assessment of typical buying scenarios and establishing definitions of dynamic sales processes that align to buyer preferences.

Aligning Training

After establishing dynamic sales process definitions and conducting assessments for each sales role, identifying the most relevant training, coaching, and skills development requirements becomes much easier. Training for developing necessary situational fluency, for execution of each of the three sales personae (i.e., Micro-Marketer, Visualizer, and Value Driver), and for use of enabling technologies, job aids, and tools can be constructed into a focused curriculum by role.

We are strong proponents of formal certification of sales mastery—a defined program where sellers demonstrate they've fully understood and can execute required competencies consistently, as evaluated by their managers out in the field. The use of a learning management system to track and manage achievement of sales mastery certification can facilitate administration and encourage broad adoption.

Top-performing sales organizations enable their sellers to receive "prioritized competency infusion." By this we mean they are providing exactly what each seller needs at the exact time the seller needs it to fully develop mastery of essential competencies for the selling role. Compare this approach to traditional monolithic method training, which gathers everyone in a generic training event where they are bombarded with topics in hope that some of it will sink in and make a difference . . . eventually. It is certainly easier to use monolithic, one-size-fits-all training approaches, but they are not very efficient. Learning and development that are tuned to the specific needs of each individual seller are more relevant to the learner and more likely to be put into practice, which is the first step toward mastery.

Learning as Transformation

Organizations that treat training as an individually transformative experience employ a 10-20-70 philosophy—that is, 10 percent of content in a training program is provided through formal instruction, 20 percent is from observing and giving feedback to peers, and 70 percent is experiential through real-world application.

Ideally, the 10 percent for instruction should be a blended learning program, combining some prework, live instructor-led sessions, and follow-up content reinforcement using online resources. The 20 percent for social learning is an opportunity to learn from peers and share best practices and results. The 70 percent for experiential learning is characterized by on-the-job application of concepts, where desired behavior changes should be observed by either trainers, management, or both and measured against how they contribute to specific business results.

Right People: Talent Assessment and Analytics

Organizations achieve optimal results when they embrace standards for how to engage with customers, as defined in dynamic sales processes. Before you can assess, develop, or enable your team, you must define what the gold standard looks like for each sales or supporting role that plays a part in your dynamic sales process. You can formulate a gold standard by asking, for each of the roles in your sales organization, what skills, attitudes, and behaviors do they need to demonstrate? How good do they have to be at each?

An effective sales talent assessment strategy is essential to implementing the Collaborative Sale—and it entails four key components, illustrated in Figure 9.3.

Defining Sales Competencies

In Part II of this book, we introduced the essential competencies required for each of the three personae of *The Collaborative Sale*. While these competencies provide an excellent baseline, each organization will also need to consider types of sales and management roles, and refine definitions of what the gold standard looks like for each role and persona. Different sales positions will require different competencies and levels of proficiency for each. Developing a complete graphic

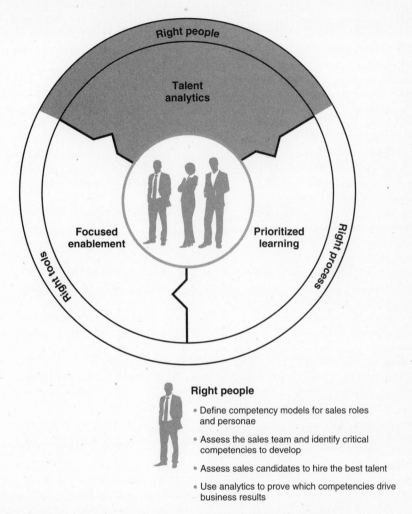

Figure 9.3   Four Key Components for Right People for the Collaborative Sale

profile of the essential competencies and mastery levels—also called a *competency skyline*—makes it easier to understand what kinds of abilities are needed for each sales-related job, as illustrated in Figure 9.4.

Micromarketer

	Situational knowledge	Capability knowledge	Demand creation	Problem identification	Technical skills	Social utilization
Expert			▨			▨
Proficient	▨		▨			▨
Application	▨		▨	▨	▨	▨
Foundational	▨	▨	▨	▨	▨	▨

Visualizer

	Communication skills	Sales conversation skills	Opportunity qualification	Competitive skills	Relationship building	Customer focus
Expert		▨				▨
Proficient	▨	▨	▨		▨	▨
Application	▨	▨	▨	▨	▨	▨
Foundational	▨	▨	▨	▨	▨	▨

Value driver

	Value identification	Financial acumen	Risk management	Value articulation	Technical skills	Communication skills
Expert	▨	▨		▨		▨
Proficient	▨	▨	▨	▨		▨
Application	▨	▨	▨	▨	▨	▨
Foundational	▨	▨	▨	▨	▨	▨

Figure 9.4 Example of a Competency Skyline for a Business Development Manager Position

Assessing Sales Teams

With defined gold standards for each sales role and persona, you can then assess the current sales team relative to the standards. This will identify competencies that need to be improved in order to support a successful transition to the Collaborative Sale. Some sellers might be gold, but most will be silver or bronze. By focusing specific learning and enablement capabilities to develop and enhance needed competencies, the highest return on investment can be realized.

When assessing the sales team, we recommend measuring four sets of key factors for each person:

1. *Potential* as measured by innate traits and behaviors (sales DNA) specific to the role and personae.

2. *Knowledge* as measured by understanding of the competencies necessary for the role.

3. *Application* as measured by an individual's ability to use his or her knowledge to perform functions required by the role and personae.

4. *Performance* as measured by how the personae has historically performed against the gold-standard benchmarks.

Taken together, these four factors enable the identification of any gaps that would inhibit achievement of a successful implementation of the Collaborative Sale, at both individual and collective levels. Our advice is not to assess once; rather, assess periodically to track progress and determine if any new remediation actions are required to close any gaps.

Assessing Sales Candidates

When recruiting and selecting new sales talent, managers should use the established gold standards for each sales role and persona for evaluation of candidates. Too often, a company's hiring process relies heavily on subjective information with little to no objective data. Instead, this process should leverage quantitative measures of the four key factors (i.e., potential, knowledge, application, and performance) to identify individuals who meet the gold standard—or demonstrate the potential to meet it. By assessing qualified sales candidates, you will better understand what kind of training and development investment will be needed to bring that seller to gold standard performance.

Establishing a consistent structure for sales talent evaluation and selection can also help to maintain objectivity in the hiring process.

Using Analytics to Connect Competencies to Business Results

By measuring individual seller results and comparing them against seller competency levels, the linkage between performance and specific knowledge, skills, and abilities can be confirmed. This provides another data set to drive improvements in learning and development curricula and related reinforcement resources and for refinement of role profiles for use in sales talent selection.

Figure 9.5 outlines the relationships between competency levels of required sales knowledge or skill, associated behaviors, and relevant outcomes (i.e., both leading and lagging indicators of sales performance). With advanced analytics, these assumptions can be tested and quantified, thus facilitating decisions based on facts, instead of on assumptions.

Recent advances in data capture and storage technologies and statistical analysis have culminated in the application of "big data" analytical methods across many industries. Using more advanced statistical

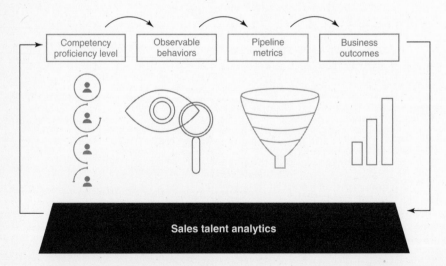

Figure 9.5   Using Sales Talent Analytics to Connect to Results

analysis methodologies, it is possible not only to create predictive models (i.e., regression analysis) but even to draw cause-and-effect inferences using more advanced structural equations modeling (SEM).

Practically speaking, SEM allows for a much higher level of confidence above and beyond what a correlation can show. For example, shark attacks and ice cream sales are correlated but have nothing to do with each other—and ice cream company executives could make horrible strategic decisions based on that correlation analysis. An argument for investment carries much more weight in the boardroom using SEM versus a correlation. By using these advanced analytics, organizations can make better strategic decisions about prioritization and investments in its sales force (e.g., hiring, training).

Right Tools: Focused Enablement

The right tools can help sellers to execute the Collaborative Sale more effectively. More importantly, they can also help sellers to differentiate themselves with buyers.

For example, collaborative interaction with Buyer 2.0 can be encouraged and facilitated by providing a secure online collaboration site, reserved for that particular buyer organization. This site may be a secure wiki, a Microsoft SharePoint page, a dedicated customer portal, or similar technology—all designed to encourage transparency and sharing of relevant information between sellers and buyers.

A secure online collaboration site differentiates the seller, as it provides full transparency over every aspect of the buyer-seller interaction. In short, it makes the collaborative seller of higher value to the buyer, and much easier to do business with.

We agree with Forrester Research's concern about "random acts of sales support"[2]—the practice of essentially throwing enablement tools

---

[2]Scott Santucci, "Getting Zen about Sales Enablement," *Forrester Blogs*, Forrester Research, February 6, 2013. Accessed December 1, 2013, at http://blogs .forrester.com/scott_santucci/13-02-06-getting_zen_about_sales_enablement.

at sales forces to see which ones stick. This is surprisingly common as the number of affordable "Sales 2.0" tools and applications,[3] designed to assist sellers with connecting to and engaging with buyers, has increased dramatically since 2009.[4]

In our experience with global companies, applying a coherent approach to sales enablement is more critical to successful implementation, as measured by seller adoption and usage, than the actual technologies introduced. Sales organizations can improve the utility gained from sales enablement tools investments by establishing an implementation framework organized into five key components, shown in Figure 9.6.

Implementing Adaptive Process and Methodology Automation

One way to help sellers apply the personae of *The Collaborative Sale* consistently is to make the tools of the methodology easy to access and reflexive for daily use. To accomplish this, providing the right tools at the right times can make consistent use of the methodology more intuitive and natural for sellers. With integrated support of a dynamic sales process within a customer relationship management (CRM) application, sellers can use the system as a source of guidance and useful job aids, as well as a standard record of opportunity status for management.

Many CRM systems handle sales opportunity management using automated work flows that can be cumbersome and difficult to understand, and therefore require significant amounts of user training. We

---

[3]Anneke Seley and Brent Holloway, *Sales 2.0: Improve Business Results Using Innovative Sales Practices and Technology* (Hoboken, NJ: John Wiley & Sons, 2009).

[4]"... [T]here are over 2,000 Sales 2.0 solutions on the market," from "Sales Productivity: The Quick Guide to Sales Technology You Can Buy with Your Credit Card," *TOPO HQ Blog*, TOPO HQ, August 12, 2013. Accessed December 6, 2013.

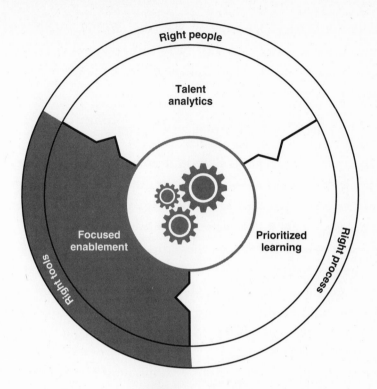

Right people

Talent
analytics

Focused
enablement

Prioritized
learning

Right tools

Right process

Right tools

- Implement adaptive process and methodology automation
- Provide contextual knowledge management aligned with process
- Leverage sales intelligence and social media
- Utilize collaborative value-justification tools throughout the sales cycle
- Explore big data opportunities to leapfrog traditional practices

Figure 9.6   Five Key Components for Right Tools for the Collaborative Sale

have found that if the CRM user interface provides a visual reference for dynamic sales process—literally, a picture of the process and an indication of the seller's progression through it—it is much easier for sellers to understand. Just as shopping malls use maps to help shoppers navigate to stores, sellers and managers need to see a clear "You are here" indicator in sales opportunities. With this kind of user interface, use of the dynamic sales process becomes a natural aspect of every opportunity. Figure 9.7 shows an example of this approach.

Providing Knowledge in Context, Aligned with Process

In the sport of American football, every team has a book containing its strategies and tactics for each play of the game, defined for different scenarios. These playbooks are visual diagrams and explanations of who needs to do what tasks where and in what sequence, in order for the team to succeed. Similarly, sales teams can use visual playbooks to better understand the buyer's state and what the seller should do in that situation. There is one major difference between a sports team's playbook and a sales team's playbook, however—the seller is not competing with the buyer, but seeking to engage and collaborate with the buyer to enable mutual success.

CRM systems can be repositories for dynamic sales process playbooks that describe effective seller practices for different situations, and within the buying stages reflected in each. While most organizations simply define sales process stages within their CRM so they can classify opportunity progress, more is needed. A dynamic sales process playbook provides more practical guidance and utility to sellers, as it helps them know what to do to better align with Buyer 2.0.

Sales organizations should augment mainstream CRM systems with intuitive, dynamic sales process playbooks that reinforce both the learning and the application of effective sales methodology, such as the Collaborative Sale. Ideally, such an enhancement enables each seller and manager to mutually agree where each opportunity is within a dynamic sales process. The playbook should describe recommended actions for each stage, including seller activities, verifiable outcomes, and job aids that will be useful for continued development of the opportunity. Sellers and managers can use this approach to facilitate

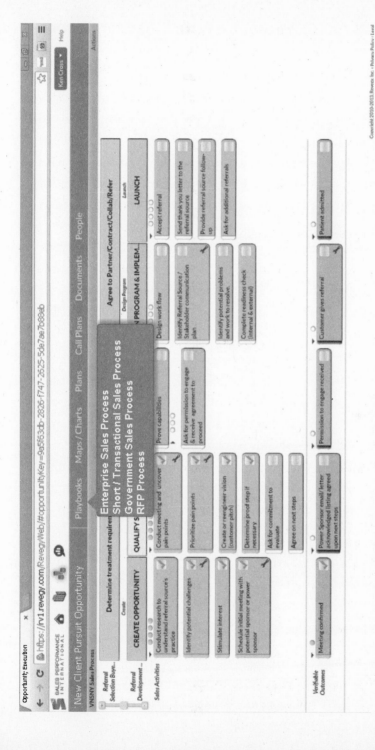

Figure 9.7 Example of a Visual Dynamic Sales Process

This example illustrates how automation of a dynamic sales process within CRM can provide seller guidance with relevant playbooks—in this case, using the Revegy application platform.

171

regular opportunity and pipeline reviews and subsequent coaching sessions.

Defining dynamic sales process playbooks within a CRM system can also accelerate sellers' mastery of the three personae of *The Collaborative Sale*. If sellers find it difficult to apply new learning to real-world scenarios, the value of that learning is greatly diminished. Dynamic sales process playbooks, linking to tools, job aids, and learning assets relevant to each stage, enable sellers to reinforce their understanding of the buyer's current state. For example, if a seller is about to enter negotiations with a buyer, the process map could provide useful links to negotiation planning tools, online training about effective negotiations, examples of job aids for negotiation execution, and so on. Dynamic sales process playbooks provide a readily understood context for access to the most relevant continual learning and sales enablement assets, as shown in Figure 9.8.

In a practical way, this approach closes gaps between learning and application of effective sales methodology. By providing the most relevant information in the context of the process, sellers are also able to access specifically what they need from collateral templates, cheat sheets, and other job aids when it is most needed. Most sales operations managers can relate to the constant battle of ensuring that their sellers have access to the latest version of presentations, contracts, proposals, and other selling resources. By linking this information within the context of the process, sellers not only know what to use, but also begin to understand when to use these tools most appropriately to collaborate more effectively with Buyer 2.0.

Leveraging Sales Intelligence and Social Media

In order to facilitate the Micro-Marketing persona, sellers should have access to information to keep them informed about customers, prospects, markets—and ongoing conversations involving all of them. As shown in Figure 9.9, contextual sales intelligence applications

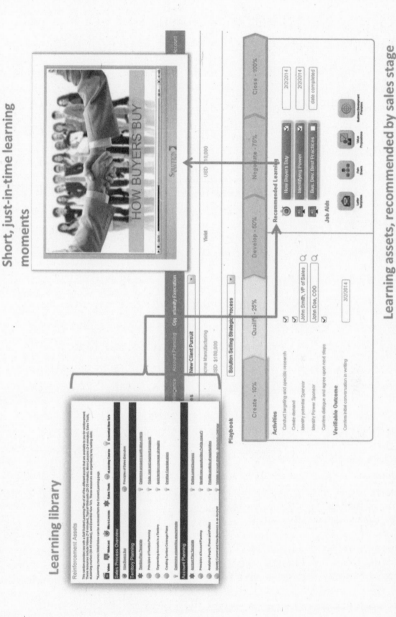

Figure 9.8   Reinforcing Methodology by Linking Dynamic Sales Process Playbooks to Learning and Enablement Assets

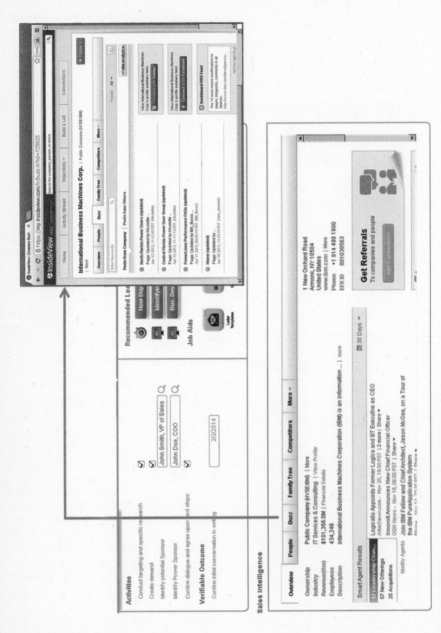

Figure 9.9   Contextual Sales Intelligence

and social media tools can help sellers with sales planning, buyer research, stimulating buyer interest, establishing and tracking buyers' business triggers, participating in networking and community groups, and other activities that are essential for successful execution of the personae of *The Collaborative Sale*.

Utilizing Collaborative Value Estimation Tools

To facilitate a seller's mastery of the Value Driver persona, collaborative online value estimation tools, such as VisualizeROI, SharkFinesse, and ROI4Sales, can also help buyers and sellers to jointly develop and agree on the value of a vision of a potential solution. The most useful value estimation tools extend beyond simply providing a return on investment (ROI) calculation. They are also platforms for communicating value throughout the buying process and fostering collaboration with Buyer 2.0. A value analysis is best determined in collaboration with a buyer.

Visualization of the quantity of value helps buyers understand the cost of the status quo. A collaborative value estimation tool that provides a graphic picture of the amount of value potential, as illustrated in Figure 9.10, enables buyers to more easily develop an accurate vision of a solution, and therefore find compelling reasons to take action.

Explore Big Data Opportunities

Big data refers to the collection and analysis of large sets of information. New tools for finding relevant insights from big data have become available, providing sales operations with potentially useful ways to identify the most effective sales practices and other untapped selling opportunities. Sales and marketing teams are now using big data for applications such as:

- Improving sales talent assessment and hiring practices, as previously described

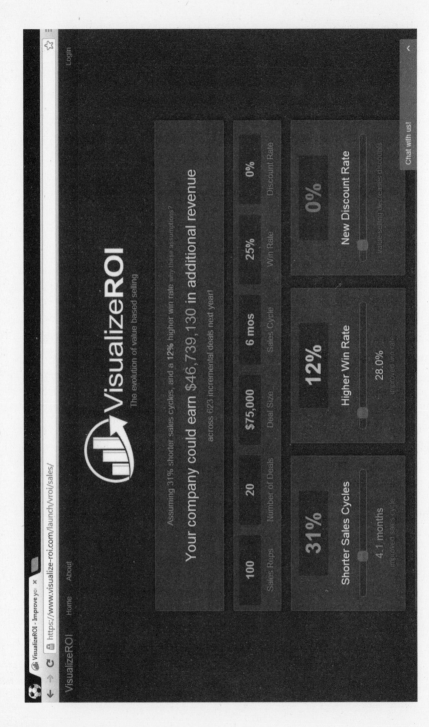

Figure 9.10   Example of a Collaborative Value Estimation Tool

- Refining Micro-Marketer targeting by identifying select peer groups that share buying characteristics

- Improving market coverage by adapting sales resource assignments to highest-potential buyer types

- Refining sales playbooks by testing selling methods applied in certain situations and linking them to empirical results

Big data analysis provides a wealth of potential competitive advantages to sales organizations that compete in markets where large collections of buyer information exist.

Committing to Success—Individually and Organizationally

Implementing *The Collaborative Sale* requires commitment. However, the business results achieved from its implementation make the effort worthwhile. There are benefits to be gained at both the individual seller level as well as organizationally. In the short term, sellers can see sales improvement through the use of specific ideas or tools in *The Collaborative Sale*. This individual effort does not require an organizational-level change.

An organizational commitment to using *The Collaborative Sale* by developing the right process, the right people, and the right tools will maximize adoption and application and thereby produce sustainable improvements in business results.

EPILOGUE

"THE STORY" CONTINUES ...

J on's plane landed in San Francisco. As it was taxiing to the gate, he switched his phone from airplane mode. It jingled as a series of voice mails, texts, and e-mails loaded.

A text from Nancy shouldn't have surprised him. Those directors watched the pipeline like hawks. He'd wait until he had more privacy than a whole plane of business travelers could provide before calling her. Scrolling through his e-mails, he was shocked to see this e-mail from the insurance broker:

> Attached is the executed letter of intent to license ExyRisk. I believe we've captured our mutual intent here, with a hat tip to your collaborative approach throughout the process, which certainly greased the skids. Now the fun begins as the lawyers attempt to ruin the deal for both of us. Let's not let that happen.

Jon forwarded the e-mail to Nancy with a cover note:

> Wow. He's had this for only three days and got the CEO's signature. I hope this is an omen for many deals to come. Thanks for the kick in the pants. Call at your first opportunity to debrief.

His phone rang before he reached the Mascone convention center. He answered, "Hey, Nancy, sweet deal, huh?"

"Great job, Jon," she said. "So great, as a matter of fact, that I've got a lead on a Brazilian company with a similar need. I assume your passport is current?"

Jon smiled. "How soon do I leave?"

AFTERWORD

Thanks for reading *The Collaborative Sale*. We sincerely want to know what you thought of the book and the concepts. Please send your feedback or any questions to: www.thecollaborativesale.com or www.spisales.com.

A dear friend recently gave me a book that I fell in love with. Don't laugh, but it is an illustrated children's book—*The Spyglass* by Richard Paul Evans with illustrations by Jonathan Linton.[1] In addition to the wonderful story line and illustrations, what also made it special was the personal handwritten sentiment inside. It said, "To a wonderful friend and visionary."

My friend wrote the inscription before she read *The Collaborative Sale*, and it touched me deeply. The connection she was making has to do with the story of *The Spyglass* and how she sees me as the founder and CEO of Sales Performance International. You see, in the book, an entire kingdom fell into ruin because neither the king nor the people had a vision for their lives. The people of the kingdom were not just poor in terms of material possessions; they were also poor of spirit.

To make things worse, to the east of this unhappy land was a beautiful kingdom with great farms, glorious gardens, cathedrals, and castles. Night and day, the breeze from the east blew the sounds and smells of this glorious kingdom to their land, reminding them of just

---

[1] Richard Paul Evans and Jonathan Linton, *The Spyglass: A Story of Faith* (New York: Simon & Schuster for Young Readers, 2000).

how poor they actually were. The king did not want to leave his castle because he didn't want to hear the complaints.

Then one day there was a knock on the king's door from a man carrying nothing but a spyglass. The man was a Visualizer and through the spyglass he helped the king see great farms, glorious gardens, cathedrals, and castles once again in his own kingdom. "Is this a trick?" the king asked. "No," said the Visualizer, "you have seen what might be; now go make it so."

The king rode throughout the kingdom sharing the spyglass, each time saying, "You have seen what might be; now go make it so." Though there were some who would not believe what they saw through the spyglass, the majority of the people did. That same year there was a plentiful harvest, and the gardens and a majestic cathedral were once again raised.

After the second year, the Visualizer returned and said, "You have done well. I cannot tarry—I only came back for my spyglass." At this the king frowned and asked the Visualizer to leave the spyglass in exchange for all of the king's gold. "You have spoken wisely," said the Visualizer, "for the gift of the spyglass is worth more than all the gold in the royal coffers. But keep your gold; you no longer need the spyglass. You are now a Visualizer; you can see without it." The king was in disbelief and asked, "How is this possible?" The Visualizer placed his hand on the king's shoulder and said with a smile, "You have seen what might be. Now go make it so."

In *The Collaborative Sale*, you have seen what might be. It's now up to you. Go make it so!

Keith Eades
CEO and Founder
Sales Performance International

APPENDIX

Essential Competencies for *The Collaborative Sale*

The three personae of *The Collaborative Sale* require sellers to possess or develop a number of key competencies—knowledge, skills, or abilities that enable them to perform the required behaviors for each persona. Managers implementing *The Collaborative Sale* should look for evidence of these competencies in any potential new hire, and examine what competencies need to be developed in existing sellers on staff.

Some of these competencies overlap, especially those required for situational fluency (see Chapter 3), which is the foundation of each of the three personae.

Sales Performance International (SPI) offers assessments that measure sellers' levels of these competencies. For more information, go to www.spisales.com.

Micro-Marketer Competencies

In order to execute successfully the actions needed to fulfill the Micro-Marketer persona, a seller must possess the following essential characteristics, knowledge, skills, and abilities:

- **Situational knowledge**—understands the buyer's industry, job roles, areas of responsibility, and common business issues.
- **Capability knowledge**—understands product and service solutions, and how they address customer business issues or capitalize on potential opportunities.

183

- **Demand creation**—creates and uses business development messaging for generating demand, providing thought leadership, and stimulating buyer interest.

- **Problem needs identification**—identifies buyers' business drivers for change within a targeted market, organization, prospect, or opportunity.

- **Communication skills**—has ability to express points of view clearly, both orally and in written form.

- **Networking and relationship-building skills**—is able to build productive social bonds with customers and buyers; builds, maintains, and leverages mutually beneficial business relationships.

- **Social media utilization**—uses social media tools to expand seller's knowledge and to interact with and influence buyers.

- **Technical skills**—is able to use appropriate technology to participate in social web and online customer conversations, as well as any supporting Micro-Marketer technologies, such as a marketing automation system.

- **Planning and organizational skills**—can use structured processes and methods to identify a logical sequence of events and activities required to achieve an intended goal or result.

Visualizer Competencies

In order to execute successfully the actions needed to fulfill the Visualizer persona, a seller must possess the following essential characteristics, knowledge, skills, and abilities:

- **Situational knowledge**—understands the buyer's industry, job roles, areas of responsibility, and common business issues.

- **Capability knowledge**—understands product and service solutions, and how they address customer business issues or capitalize on potential opportunities.

- **Communication skills**—has ability to express points of view clearly, both orally and in written form.

- **Sales conversation skills**—collaboratively diagnoses buyer problems or potential opportunities; creates, expands, or reengineers visions of solutions; develops mutual agreement with buyers on capabilities needed.

- **Opportunity qualification**—applies guiding standards to assess the correct buyer state, strength of buyer vision, and quality of a sales opportunity, and then make engagement and prioritization decisions.

- **Competitive skills**—evaluates competitive positions and executes appropriate strategies and tactics to win.

- **Relationship-building skills**—is able to build productive social bonds with customers and buyers; builds, maintains, and leverages mutually beneficial business relationships.

- **Customer focus**—keeps the customer foremost in mind; advocates for the customer's best interests.

Value Driver Competencies

In order to execute successfully the actions needed to fulfill the Value Driver persona, a seller must possess the following essential characteristics, knowledge, skills, and abilities:

- **Situational knowledge**—understands the buyer's industry, job roles, areas of responsibility, and common business issues.

- **Capability knowledge**—understands product and service solutions, and how they address customer business issues or capitalize on potential opportunities.

- **Value identification and articulation**—determines scope and impact of buyer problems or potential opportunities; identifies, quantifies, and communicates the tangible results of proposed solutions; can identify or create compelling reasons to act based on value.

- **Financial acumen**—understands buyers' financial statements, key performance measures, and how their decisions will affect value creation.

- **Risk management skills**—can relate to and understand buyers' risks at both the individual level and the organizational level; can take appropriate actions to mitigate buyer risks.

- **Technical skills**—is able to use appropriate technology to operate business impact and value analysis estimation tools, such as online collaborative value calculators and specialized Excel worksheets.

- **Customer focus**—keeps the customer foremost in mind; advocates for the customer's best interests; can anticipate potential solution transition and implementation issues for specific customers and recommend appropriate actions and resources to address those issues.

- **Communication skills**—has ability to express points of view clearly, both orally and in written form.

Additional Collaborative Selling Tools

The Collaborative Sale describes several tools and job aids to help sellers collaborate with Buyer 2.0 to progress to a buying decision. In addition to those tools described in earlier chapters, we show some additional tools that may be helpful here. Readers can find downloadable templates for these tools at www.thecollaborativesale.com or at www.spisales.com.

Results Story

A story that describes a situation similar to that of the buyer and expresses the results for solving the problem or capitalizing on an otherwise missed opportunity (e.g., the potential "pain" of the buyer) enables Buyer 2.0 to envision how they might realize the same kind of benefits. It is a very good tool for helping the Micro-Marketer persona to stimulate the curiosity of a targeted buyer. The story does not have to name a specific customer or reference; a general job title and industry are sufficient. The key is to share specific, quantitative results for addressing the buyer. Figure A.1 shows the format for a good results story.

Target Buyer Profile

When a seller identifies a potential buyer, the seller should develop the right level of situational fluency before trying to engage. This means understanding that buyer's organization, critical business issues or potential opportunities (possible pains), business drivers, and related factors (reasons for the pains), key players (who owns the pains), and a hypothesis of the capabilities that may help the buyer to address the issues or capitalize on an opportunity (a prospective vision of a solution). This tool can be used by a Micro-Marketer persona to help develop sufficient situational fluency to approach a target buyer, or by a Visualizer persona to help formulate an initial vision of a potential solution. Figure A.2 shows the format for a useful target buyer profile.

Situation	Record the job title and history.
Critical business issue	Describe the pain of the job title.
Reason(s)	Describe the reason or reasons that led to the pain.
Capability(ies) when, who, what	Describe, in the words of the client, the capabilities needed.
We provided...	...this capability.
Result	Describe the results and time frame, and ensure that the results address the pain.

Figure A.1   Results Story Format

Target buyer	
Background	
Offerings	
Market analysis	
Key financials	
Competition	
Key players	
Potential critical business issues	
Capabilities needed (initial vision)	

Figure A.2   Target Buyer Profile

Assumed Value Estimate

An effective tool for stimulating interest with buyers is a value proposition or value estimate. This tool expresses an initial, assumed estimate of value for addressing a potential problem or opportunity. This tool is often used by the Value Driver persona early in the buying process to stimulate interest or later in the buying process if entering late. In documenting their assumptions, sellers should not obsess about being exceptionally precise with this tool—it is designed to stimulate interest or further a conversation with the buyer. Ultimately, the goal is to collaborate further with the buyer and reach mutual agreement on the real value. Figure A.3 shows the format for a good assumed value estimate.

Differentiation Grid

The Visualizer persona must be prepared to engage with the buyer in conversations that provide insight and value. To that end, sellers must understand what unique differentiators they can bring to help develop a compelling vision in collaboration with the buyer. The differentiation grid is a simple exercise that helps develop that understanding based on the uniqueness and value of potential solution capabilities for the

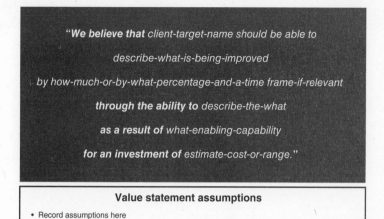

Figure A.3   Assumed Value Estimate Format

buyer. By evaluating and charting each of these capabilities, the Visualizer can focus on those solution components that provide the most value and that also help to differentiate the vision from alternatives. Figure A.4 provides a template for the differentiation grid exercise.

Sales Conversation Prompter

The Visualizer persona engages in conversations with buyers to create, enhance, or reengineer visions of a potential solution. The collaborative sales conversation structure described in Chapter 5 provides a method for sellers to execute dialogues with buyers that encourage collaboration toward a mutually agreed vision of a solution. Soliciting the buyer perspective is relatively easy for sellers—they only have to ask open questions. Sellers should be prepared to share their own perspectives, so that they can ask insightful questions and demonstrate situational fluency. The sales conversation prompter tool enables the Visualizer persona to accomplish this. It can be used to prepare for vision creation, vision enhancement, or vision reengineering conversations. Figure A.5 shows a sales conversation prompter template.

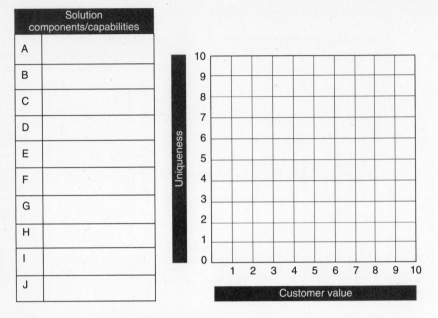

Figure A.4   Differentiation Grid

Problem or potential opportunity	
Person (job title and industry)	

Reasons	Capabilities
A	A
B	B
C	C

Figure A.5   Sales Conversation Prompter

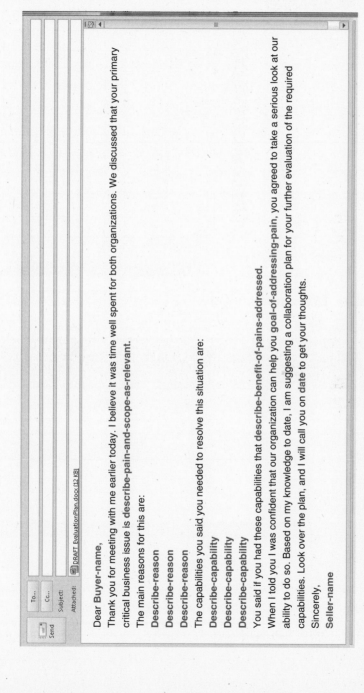

Figure A.6 Buyer Communication Template

Buyer Communication

After meeting with a buyer, whether virtually or in person, sellers should confirm their alignment by sending a communication, usually an e-mail message, to the buyer. The communication should confirm the problem or potential opportunity ("pain"), the reasons for the issue, the capabilities needed, the initial value or key benefits, and agreed-upon next steps. The intent of the communication is to generate a response from the buyer; the quality of that response is a verifiable outcome showing alignment and progress with the buyer. Figure A.6 shows a template for a suitable buyer communication.

	Is it closeable today?	☑ Power to buy? ☑ Payback agreed to? ☑ Legal/Technical/Admin approvals? ☑ Collaboration Plan/Next Steps completed? ☑ Buyer has known the cost since...?
Stand 1 (plan)	Our mutually agreed-upon plan shows the kickoff of this project starting the week of **enter-date**. Is this issue worth the delay?	
Stand 2 (value)	When we calculated the value/payback, you told me that even with the investment being made the return was higher than you expected and the project would pay for itself in **time frame.** Has something changed?	
Stand 3 (pain)	The primary reason we have spent the last **number** of months together is because **describe-the-pain.** That issue is not going to go away until you gain these new capabilities. Is this still a priority for you?	

SELLER : "The only way I could do something for you is if you could do something for me."
BUYER(should ask): "Like what?"
SELLER: "Is it possible for you...(desired get)...(confirm)... ifyou can, then we are prepared to (suggested give)..."

Get	Value ←	→	Give	
1				1
2				2
3				3
Not Negotiable				
1				
2				
3				

Figure A.7   Collaborative Negotiation Worksheet

Collaborative Negotiation Worksheet

Sellers must know how to negotiate effectively in order to secure business with Buyer 2.0. By the time an opportunity is at this stage, the seller should have used the Visualizer persona to develop a clear vision of a solution in collaboration with the buyer, and also used the Value Driver persona to establish a jointly agreed estimate of value for the solution. This information can be used to prepare for a suitable negotiation that is a win-win agreement for both the buyer and the seller. An effective negotiation should be a joint collaboration exercise, instead of a conflict. The collaborative negotiation worksheet, illustrated in Figure A.7, helps sellers to prepare for a collaborative negotiation session with the buyer.

CONTRIBUTORS

Keith M. Eades

Keith is Founder and CEO of Sales Performance International (SPI), one of the largest sales improvement companies in the world. Headquartered in Charlotte, North Carolina, SPI is currently doing business in more than 50 countries.

Keith speaks regularly at industry, customer, and partner events, and he is considered one of the most knowledgeable authorities on transforming companies into world-class sales organizations. *The Collaborative Sale* is Keith's fourth book.

In 2001, Clemson University recognized Keith with the Alumni Fellow Award for his outstanding career accomplishments. He is an inaugural member of the Shapiro Center Entrepreneurial Round Table and serves on the Executive Advisory Board for the College of Business and Behavioral Sciences at Clemson.

Timothy T. Sullivan

Tim is Director of Business Development at Sales Performance International, where he works with clients to identify and develop solutions for sales performance issues. In this capacity, Tim has the unique opportunity to observe and collect best practices from many of the world's top-performing sales professionals.

The Collaborative Sale is Tim's second coauthored book with Keith Eades, the first being *The Solution Selling Fieldbook* (McGraw-Hill, 2005); he was also a contributor to *The Solution-Centric Organization* (McGraw-Hill, 2006). He contributes regularly to the *Solution Selling Blog*, found at www.solutionsellingblog.com. Tim is also a frequent speaker at industry conferences on advanced sales and marketing topics. He holds a business degree from the University of Notre Dame, and is a dedicated Fighting Irish football fan. He resides happily with his beautiful bride, Jane, in Atlanta, Georgia.

Robert Kear

Robert is Chief Marketing Officer at Sales Performance International. Before joining SPI, he served as VP of Marketing Strategy and Customer Relationship Management (CRM) Strategy for JD Edwards & Company. In 1994, he co-founded YOUcentric, an enterprise CRM software company, where as chief strategy officer he was responsible for all aspects of corporate strategy, market planning and execution, and product direction.

Robert has been a recipient of Ernst & Young's eBusiness Entrepreneur of the Year for the Carolinas. He holds advanced and undergraduate degrees in mathematics from East Carolina University.

He coauthored *The Solution-Centric Organization* with Keith Eades (McGraw-Hill, 2006).

James N. "Jimmy" Touchstone

Jimmy is Director of Learning Programs at Sales Performance International, where he leads and manages the ongoing development of the Solution Selling® methodology and suite of offerings. He created and led the development of continual learning components that make up the SellingStream™ Continual Learning program. Jimmy is an author and contributor to several professional publications. He co-authored *The Solution Selling Fieldbook* with Keith Eades and Tim Sullivan, which proves that an English degree from the UNC Charlotte can be valuable preparation for a business career. He is grateful to his wife Kelley and twins, Jacob and Jonah for their love and support.

Dave Christofaro

Dave is Sales Performance International's Director of Sales Talent Optimization. In this role, Dave leads a practice area focused on helping clients hire, develop, and retain top sales talent through the use of assessment and talent management technology.

Prior to SPI, Dave held sales and sales leadership roles in the high technology industry. With a degree in computer science from North Carolina State University, Dave began his career managing technology development projects with Accenture.

Living in Charlotte, North Carolina, Dave's first and favorite personal interest is spending time with his wife Melanie and his children Josh and Sofia.

Kenneth Cross

Ken is Director of Solution Selling Enablement at Sales Performance International. His team places SPI's learning, methodology, and tools at the fingertips of a global client base, usually within a customer relationship management (CRM) system.

Prior to his work at SPI, Ken worked in technology-based consulting, sales, and channel management roles for CRM and other technology-based companies. He once served as an on-air guest host for Bose products on the QVC network.

Ken is an active writer and frequent contributor to the *Solution Selling Blog*. A Pennsylvania native, he is a graduate of Westminster College and lives with his family in Pittsburgh.

Tamela M. Rich

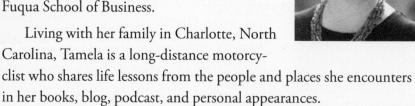

Tamela ghostwrites and edits books, articles, speeches, and presentations for an international clientele of business and financial professionals. She earned an MBA from Duke University's Fuqua School of Business.

Living with her family in Charlotte, North Carolina, Tamela is a long-distance motorcyclist who shares life lessons from the people and places she encounters in her books, blog, podcast, and personal appearances.

Tamela's 2012 book, *Live Full Throttle: Life Lessons from Friends Who Faced Cancer*, won three national (U.S.) awards. Her website is www.tamelarich.com.

INDEX